THE LANDLORD'S
RESIDENTIAL L

BY

BARRY CONNICK A.R.I.C.S.

AND

MICHAEL KROKATSIS F.P.C.S.

PROMOTED BY:

ALPHA-LETS (UK) LTD
LETTING AGENTS AND PROPERTY MANAGERS
371 GREEN LANES
LONDON N4 1DY

TEL: 0181-809 6144, FAX: 0181-800 4887

INTRODUCTION

The following guide is intended for the use of any landlord who wishes to find out how to go about letting a property. It will be found useful both by those landlords who are new to the concept of letting properties and those existing landlords who wish to keep up to date with the latest legislation.

This guide is not intended to be an in-depth law book but merely a guide to introduce the various aspects of property letting and management and to give a potential landlord an insight into the letting and management process.

The individual landlord will have to consult the appropriate professionals for a greater knowledge of the law regarding contracts and the financial/tax implications of any letting.

Whilst every care has been taken in the preparation of this guide the authors cannot be held responsible for any published inaccuracies - expert advice should always be sought for the particular situation in which the landlord finds himself.

This guide is not intended to give an authoritative interpretation of the law, but to guide the landlord and/or tenant in the right direction; if you are in any doubt regarding your legal position or obligations, your should consult a solicitor.

The legislation described in this guide is current for England and Wales. It does not apply in Scotland or Northern Ireland.

Certain terminology has been used within this guide. A brief explanation of some of this terminology is to be found as a glossary of terms.

Wherever HIS or HE has been used, read HIS/HER or HE/SHE.

CONTENTS

CONTENTS

CONTENTS

CHAPTER 1 - CAN I LET MY PROPERTY ?

There are many reasons why people let properties. These reasons are not of concern in this guide, but we will attempt to answer the many questions which arise as a consequence of letting properties.

A landlord has many obligations when letting out a property, and we will now address those with which he has a legal or moral duty to comply.

MORTGAGES

Where there is an outstanding loan with a mortgage company or bank etc., it may prove necessary to inform them of the intention to let the property. The small print of the particular loan will indicate whether this is so. If in doubt consult your mortgage broker or lender, direct.

Tenancies should not be arranged before the lender's permission has been obtained. It is most unwise to present a lender with a "fait accompli".

On request most loan companies will indicate, in writing, whether they are happy for the property to be rented. Permission will often be granted if the applicant is moving away on business or will be out of the country for a long period of time.

As a generalisation mortgage companies are not willing to allow the letting of a property with a mortgage on it, purely on speculative grounds, unless the landlord can prove that he has sufficient funds to cover most unforeseen eventualities and that he can indicate that he has enough experience to carry out the management of the property. A working capital sum of say £5,000 - £10,000 and the use of an established managing agent may be the sort of assurance the mortgage company is looking for.

In this type of circumstance the mortgage company might see the rental of the property as a business venture. It has been known for them to increase the rate of interest to that of a business rate, usually around 2 or 3 per cent above the residential rate. This is something that should be discussed with the lender and usually they will make an assessment on the actual circumstances given.

Most lenders will have some sort of application form to be completed before permission will be granted, typical questions asked will include:

- What is the reason for the proposed letting ?
- What is the period of the proposed letting ?
- Is the letting to be furnished or unfurnished ?
- Will the whole of the property be let ?

Other more specific details may be required; such as income tax details. It is currently a legal requirement for the lender to notify the Inland Revenue if a mortgaged property is let.

The requisite permission is likely to be granted only if the following conditions are met:

- The names of the tenants and the date of the commencement of the tenancy, the length of the tenancy etc. are provided.
- Confirmation that the statutory notices, in the correct form, have been served on the tenants *prior* to the commencement of the tenancy and that a valid Assured Tenancy or more likely an Assured Shorthold Tenancy has been created. The lender will be particularly keen to ensure that the Section 20 notice and the notices covering Grounds 1 and 2 of Schedule 2 of the Housing Act 1988 have been served (see section on contracts for explanations).

- The Agreement must not allow the tenant to assign, sublet or part with possession of the property.
- The tenant must not have diplomatic or any other immunity.
- The property must only be used as a domestic dwelling for residential purposes and may not be used for any business purposes whatsoever.

PLANNING CONTROLS

Many Local Authorities have strict planning controls which cover the rental of private houses. It is prudent to contact the Local Authority to find out which rules apply in your particular area.

Where properties are let out to one "household" the normal planning and fire regulations will apply. It is only in "house of multiple occupation" (H.M.O.) that the planning and fire regulations may be different.

The Housing Act 1985 defines a house in multiple occupation as "a house (or purpose built or converted flat) occupied by persons who do not form a single household"

It is often difficult to tell whether a property is an H.M.O. (or not) and to help establish this the Department of the Environment put forward the following questions in its circular 12/93 to Local Housing Authorities. The D.o.E. emphasises that each individual case should be judged on its own merits, however, these questions may be relevant when considering a property which might be an H.M.O.:

- Whether cooking facilities are separate or shared.
- Whether washing facilities are separate or shared.
- Whether occupants eat together.
- Whether cleaning is shared or carried out individually.

- Whether occupants have separate or shared contracts.
- Whether vacancies are filled by occupants or landlords.
- Whether occupants come and go frequently.

The Institution of Environmental Health Officers have gone into slightly more depth, with factors they think should be considered when trying to establish whether a property is an H.M.O., their factors are:

- Does each occupier have a separate contractual relationship with the landlord ?
- Has each occupant acquired the right to reside in the property by negotiation with the landlord only ?
- On termination of any tenancy or licence, who finds the new occupants, the landlord, or the remaining tenants ?
- Does the landlord bear the loss of rent whilst any vacancy exists within the property ? Are vacancies advertised and filled by the landlord ?
- Who has responsibility for giving notice to undesirable tenants, or for non payment of rent ?
- Is the property run by a resident landlord or head tenant as a business and for profit ?
- Are the occupants granted exclusive possession of their rooms or any parts of the house ?
- Do occupants come and go at frequent intervals or are occupancies on a long and stable basis ?
- Are there separate cooking facilities in each of the occupant's rooms or on separate floors or do occupants eat together when convenient ?
- Are washing and sanitary facilities in occupant's rooms or on separate floors ?
- Do occupants make separate arrangements for cooking and eating ?
- Do all occupants have their own separate personal cooking utensils or are they shared ?
- Is payment made to one person who provides meals on a business, board or lodging basis ?

- Does each occupant undertake his own cleaning with a landlord for common parts or is it organised between occupants on a rota basis ?

Once it has been established that a property is indeed an H.M.O., then the necessary planning and fire regulations need be applied. The D.o.E. recognise that differing H.M.O.s require differing levels of amenities and safety and so recommend that the H.M.O.s are placed in one of the following six categories (drawn up by the Institution of Environmental Health Officers), in order for these standards to be better applied.

The six categories are:-

- **Category A:** Houses occupied as individual rooms, bedsits and flatlets which are considered to have a number of rooms for exclusive occupation, not necessarily behind one door, with some sharing of amenities usually bathroom and/or toilet and maybe a kitchen. In such a house each occupancy would be separately rented.
- **Category B:** Houses occupied on a shared basis. These would normally be occupied by students where for certain activities the occupants might live as a single household unit, but for others do not. Usually the house will be let to a defined group and not individuals. The house is most likely to be shared by four or more people and although most common among students it is increasingly found by groups of people coming together in the house who share certain amenities as they wish but have certain individual facilities such as a bedroom.
- **Category C:** Houses let in lodgings, i.e. catering for lodgers on a small scale but not living as part of the main household normally with a resident owner/occupier. This is the traditional "house let in lodgings" where meals are provided in a dining-room and would be typified by a family or household who might take in a small number of

students or other individuals away from their primary place of residence.

- **Category D:** Houses generally referred to as "Hostels", "Guesthouses", "Bed and Breakfast accommodation". They will provide accommodation for people with no other permanent place of residence as distinct from a Hotel which provides accommodation for visitors to the area for a short time. This category would include Hotels and Bed and Breakfast accommodation used by Local Authorities to house homeless families, or similar establishments which provide accommodation for single people whose financial support is "state benefit" and who would otherwise be homeless. This category would include Hotels used for such accommodation even on a casual basis.
- **Category E:** Houses which are hostels and require registration under the Registered Homes Act 1984. These residential homes providing board and personal care by reason of old age, disablement, past or present dependence on alcohol or drugs, or past or present mental disorder. Unlike Category D, these houses would provide permanent accommodation for people with nowhere else to go; this would be their only home and would include a level of support not normally present within category D accommodation, which only provides a home for the "time-being".
- **Category F:** most houses or buildings which by erection or conversion contain dwellings which are self-contained and all such dwellings comprising accommodation which is behind one access door off a common area. The dwellings would normally contain all the standard amenities although it would be possible for some to be unimproved self-contained flats lacking one or more standard amenities. There would be no sharing of amenities with occupiers of other dwellings.

CHAPTER 1 - CAN I LET MY PROPERTY ?

Where it is thought that a dwelling falls within one of these categories, it is important that the Local Planning Office is contacted to establish whether increased fire and safety regulations are required. FAILURE TO DO SO MAY RESULT IN PROSECUTION.

There is currently a Government White Paper under discussion which will make it mandatory for all H.M.O.s to be registered under a national registration scheme. It is proposed that this scheme will be in force in 1997/8.

The following is extracted from two leaflets published by:

The Fire Protection Association.
140 Aldersgate Street
London EC1A 4HX

These leaflets are available free of charge from them and are entitled:
Fire Safety in Houses in Multiple Occupation:

- Guidance for tenants.
- Guidance for owners and their representatives.

According to their statistics about 600 people die and about 11000 are injured each year, in fires, in their homes; of these about a quarter of the deaths and about a third of injuries occur in houses or flats in multiple occupation.

They say the six most common accidental causes of fires in H.M.O.s are:

Accidents during cooking (about 10000 fires)
Lack of care when smoking (about 3000 fires)
Defective electrical appliances (about 1500 fires)
Careless use or disposal of matches (about 1250 fires)
Careless use of heaters (about 900 fires)

CHAPTER 1 - CAN I LET MY PROPERTY ?

Section 352 of The Housing Act 1985 gives all Local Authorities the power to ensure that landlords provide a safe living environment for their tenants. Among other things, the landlord must provide a means of escape from fire as well as "other fire precautions". These other precautions will include portable fire fighting equipment. Larger H.M.O.s may require fire alarm and detection systems. Under section 369 of the same Act, the Housing (Management of Houses in Multiple Occupation) Regulations 1990, lay down the responsibilities of managers and tenants. This will include means of escape, fire safety equipment and exit signs.

Under these regulations the manager of an H.M.O. must ensure that:

- means of escape from fire are free from obstructions;
- fire fighting equipment is maintained in good working order;
- fire alarm and detection systems installed by the landlord are maintained in good working order;
- fire exit routes are clearly signed.

The tenants must comply with any reasonable arrangements made by the manager and generally co-operate to allow these duties to be met.

Where there are breaches of these Regulations they can be enforced by the Environmental Health Department of the Local Authority. In larger H.M.O.s (three stories or more with a total floor area exceeding 500 m2) the Local Authority has a statutory duty to ensure compliance.

The enforcement for smaller H.M.O.s is at the discretion of the Local Authority.

Some Local Authorities have schemes to register H.M.O.s and conduct regular inspections.

The stairways of an H.M.O. will normally need additional fire protection and the doors onto the stairway will usually be self closing and give at least 30 minutes fire protection. This will give a protected means of escape to the occupants.

Minimal fire precautions, such as smoke and carbon monoxide detectors should be installed in any rented property, regardless of whether it is an H.M.O., or not.

THE FURNITURE AND FURNISHINGS (FIRE) (SAFETY) REGULATION 1988 + AMENDMENTS

The following regulations apply to persons who hire out furniture as part of a business. This includes persons who let furnished accommodation.
From March 1993, furniture (whether new or second hand) which is additional to or in replacement of existing furniture in accommodation let prior to this date must comply with all the fire resistance requirements.
From March 1993, all furniture (except furniture made before 1950) included in accommodation which is let for the first time from this date must meet all the fire resistance requirements.
Any furniture not meeting the fire resistance requirements can continue to be supplied in accommodation until December 1996, provided that it was included in the letting of the same accommodation prior to 1 March 1993.
Where items contain upholstery, "furniture" may include items such as: beds, mattresses, headboards, sofa-beds etc.

The following is an interpretation of the legislation by the Department of Trade and Industry:

- The regulations apply to the actual supplier of the furniture in the course of business. This could apply either to landlord or agent, depending on the capacity in which the agent acts for the landlord.

- If the landlord employs the agent to find a tenant for the property and to manage an agreement for its letting, but the actual agreement is between the landlord and the tenant , then in such a case the supply is undertaken by the landlord as principal and he would be liable if he is letting in the course of business. He would not be liable if it is his own home he is letting.

The trading standards officer of the Local Authority will enforce the regulations.
FAILURE TO COMPLY IS A CRIMINAL OFFENCE.

Copies of the regulations can be obtained from:

HMSO Publications,
PO Box 276
London SW8 5DT.

Copies of "A Guide to Furniture and Furnishings (Fire) (Safety) Regulations" can be obtained from:

The Consumer Safety Unit
Department of Trade and Industry,
Room 302, 10-18 Victoria Street,
London SW1H ONN.

ELECTRICAL EQUIPMENT (SAFETY) REGULATIONS 1994

These regulations came into force on 9th January 1995. They cover the supply of electrical equipment (which includes landlords supplying electrical equipment in the course of letting) with a working voltage of between 50 to 1000 volts.

The regulations require:

- That all equipment is safe for use.

- That all necessary instructions (in English) are available.

Therefore it is recommended that all electrical equipment is checked by a qualified engineer.

Further information can be obtained from:-

HMSO Publications Centre
P O Box 276
London SW8 5DT

Tel: 0171 873 0022

FAILURE TO COMPLY COULD LEAD TO A FINE OF £5000.00 OR SIX MONTHS IMPRISONMENT, OR BOTH.

GAS SAFETY REGULATIONS

The Gas Safety (Installation and Use) Regulations 1994, came into effect on 31 October 1994. The main points of the regulations are as follows:

- The regulations apply to residential properties let or tenancies not exceeding 7 years including periodic tenancies e.g. monthly or weekly lets.
- Landlords are responsible for maintaining (in a safe condition) all gas appliances, flues and their pipework within the properties that they let.
- There is a specific duty to ensure that each appliance and its flue is checked for safety on (at least) an annual basis.
- These tests must be carried out by an approved installer; currently only CORGI members are approved for this purpose.
- The first test should have been carried out within the year to 31 October 1995.
- Landlords must keep a certified record of these tests, and defects that were found and any remedial action taken.

- This record must be made available for the tenant to view on request.
- These obligations extend to portable gas appliances (e.g. LPG appliances).
- The code of practice issued by the Health and Safety Executive states that where the landlord does not manage the property himself the management agreement between the landlord and the managing agent should specify who is responsible for maintaining the gas appliances and keeping the records of it.
- Where a gas appliance is owned by the tenant (who would be responsible for its maintenance), the landlord would still be responsible for the maintenance of its installation pipe work.

FAILURE TO COMPLY WITH THE REGULATIONS IS A CRIMINAL OFFENCE.

INSURANCES

BUILDINGS

It is advisable to check with the company who covers the building insurance to ascertain whether the cover is affected by the renting of the premises.

For your own protection the enquiry must be in writing and you should keep a copy of the reply.

There have been many instances where insurance companies have refused to pay out on claims because they have not been notified that the premises are let.

Insurance cover can be restricted where the property is rented out.

In some cases the property may not be acceptable to a specific insurer; where, for example, the property is let out to a Local Authority, students, tenants receiving Housing Benefit or multiple single sharers etc.

Where a landlord owns several properties he should consider combining all of these premises under a single "Residential Property Owners" block policy,

which will provide the widest cover at an economic price.
It is wise to include Public Liability cover within your building insurance policy as this will protect the property owner against any claim for injury to third parties. Check with your insurer for further details.

For those who need help with this type of insurance, please contact:

Alpha-Lets (UK) Ltd, on 0181 800 4313

who will be able to get competitive quotations from various sources for such insurance. These sources include Winter Richmund who have the popular LETsure building insurance policy (underwritten by Cornhill Insurance) and I.P.S. Insurance Brokers who have "block agreements" direct with underwriters.
Certain criteria may have to be met to enjoy these competitive premiums. In certain circumstances they may require the use of a professional property managing agent and loadings may be levied for the number of tenants and the location of the premises.

LANDLORD'S CONTENTS
Where the premises are let out on a furnished basis, the landlord may want to arrange a policy to cover his contents.
Cover on some buildings policies can be extended to include landlord's fixtures and furnishings. Check with you insurance broker whether this is possible prior to taking out separate contents insurance.

A landlord's contents policy would only cover the landlord's property and would not provide cover to the tenant's possessions. It is not possible for the tenants to insure the landlord's contents as they would not have an "insurable interest".

CHAPTER 1 - CAN I LET MY PROPERTY ?

Winter Richmund are able to offer their LETsure landlord's contents policy which will cover:- Theft, malicious damage, public liability, burst pipes and other such perils. Minimum security precautions may apply for certain tenant types and areas. The scheme is rated on the property post-code and the number of bedrooms. Please contact:

Alpha-Lets (UK) Ltd, on 0181 800 4313

for a quote on all Winter Richmund policies.

TENANT'S CONTENTS

Tenants of unfurnished or partly furnished premises, where there are only one or two occupiers of the home, are usually able to obtain standard home insurance cover, without any special terms or conditions.

Where there are several tenants at the same premises, or the premises are rented as furnished, specialist advice is require to ensure that the policy provides the correct cover.

There is a policy available from "Entertainment and Leisure" which is a personal possession policy and is specifically aimed at young people, students, nurses or anyone else living in: digs, flats, bedsits, shared accommodation, halls of residence and the like.

Winter Richmund have a tenant's contents insurance, which is similar in cover to their landlord's contents mentioned above but with additional cover for accidental damage to high risk items such as T.V.s and computers. It also covers replacement of locks following theft of keys. Tenants may take an optional extension to cover "all risks" on items taken out of the property with world-wide cover. This scheme is also rated on post-code and number of bedrooms. For further details contact:

Alpha-Lets (UK) Ltd, on 0181 800 4313.

LEGAL/RENT PROTECTION
Where the property is rented out with an Assured Shorthold Tenancy Agreement it is possible to arrange one of a number of Legal/Rent Protection insurance policies.

Four such policies are available from Winter Richmund and these offer differing levels of protection for differing premiums. These are Winter Richmund Gold, Winter Richmund MLLP, LETsure Plus and LETsure Legal Protection. For further information on these policies contact:

Alpha-Lets (UK) Ltd, on 0181 800 4313.

TAX IMPLICATIONS

"The money derived from letting a property is income that MUST be declared for taxation purposes"

There are strict rules laid down by the Inland Revenue regarding the renting of properties. These rules are constantly changing and will vary according to your personal circumstances. It is therefore vital that you contact your local Tax Office for the latest regulations.

Please note that penalties for late or non-disclosure of this income to the Inland Revenue can be far harsher under the new "self-assessment" rules, than they were under the old system.

The telephone number and address of your local Tax Office should be in your local phone book under "Inland Revenue". Most offices are open from 10am to 4pm, Monday to Friday.

CHAPTER 1 - CAN I LET MY PROPERTY ?

RENTING IN YOUR MAIN RESIDENCE

Where you rent a furnished room in your own home the following rules apply. These rules came into force from 6 April 1992.

- Where the annual rent is less than £3250, Tax is NOT payable.
- Where you do not receive a tax return, you do not even need to inform your tax office of this income, if it falls below £3250 per annum.
- Where you do receive a tax return, just tick the box to confirm that the rental income is £3250 per annum or less.
- Where the rent is greater than £3250 per annum you can choose one of the following:
  1. Paying tax on the total profit you make from letting the room (see later for list of allowable expenses)
  2. Paying tax on the amount of rent over £3250.

  Choose which ever method is most advantageous to you.

RENTING WHERE NOT YOUR MAIN RESIDENCE

Where you rent all or part of a house which is not your main residence the rental income MUST be declared to the Inland Revenue. Careful note should be made of all rent received and where possible you should keep the receipts of any expenses to be claimed. A detailed statement of all rents received should be sent where these rents exceed £15,000 per annum.

ALLOWABLE EXPENSES

Certain expenses can be offset against rental income before it is taxed. Although the following is not an exhaustive list, the main items are:-

- Repair, maintenance and redecorating expenses during the rental contract.
- Professional fees for any of the above.
- Property management fees, rent collection fees, advertising costs, legal and accountancy costs etc.

Claims Office (FICO) for approval to have their rents paid to them before deduction of tax and to settle any liability directly with the Inland Revenue. The agent will be informed accordingly and can then pay the rent over to the landlord without deduction.

In cases where there is no managing agent the tenant does not have to deduct tax if the rent does not exceed £100 per week (or £100 per tenant where there are joint tenants).

For this purpose "agent" is widely defined. It can include a relation or friend who is looking after the property as well as a professional managing agent.

You have been warned ! If you pay rent directly to a landlord living abroad, or if you are helping a landlord who lives abroad, you might find that the Inland Revenue classes you as a "managing agent", which will make you liable for the tax due! - Ignorance will NOT exempt you from any tax liability !!

For further information on any of the above, consult your Local Tax Office, your accountant or:-

George Christodoulou BA(Hons) ACCA
Gilchrists (Certified Accountants and Registered Auditors)
West Hill House
6 Swains Lane
Highgate
London N6 6QU

Tel: 0171 482 4212
Fax: 0171 267 4382

CHAPTER 1 - CAN I LET MY PROPERTY ?

CHAPTER 2 - MARKET RENTS

SOURCES OF INFORMATION

Having decided that it is possible for the property to be let, the next step is to establish a market rent. There are many considerations to be taken into account when doing this. One of the simplest ways is to contact a local Letting Agent. There are now many agencies which have been set up for Letting and Property Management and a look along your local "High Street" will usually reveal any number of them.
Most Estate Agents will now combine both letting and management functions along with the selling of properties.
It is usual for these agencies to provide free valuations and this will be a good place to start, as they will have a good basic knowledge of the area and of the localised letting market.
It must be stressed that a "local" agent be used (or at least someone who is familiar with the area) as it is common for rental levels to vary from area to area, street to street, and even from one end of a street to another, dependant on the locality. This type of variation occurs mainly in larger cities where "the right address" is something that has to be paid for.

In some cases Letting Agents provide free letting lists and these can be an invaluable source of information for rental levels.

Local newspapers often carry a specialised rental section and these can also help to establish a level of rent.

Other useful publications are:

- Loot or similar "free-ad" papers, available in certain areas.

- Newspapers carrying "classified" adverts such as the Evening Standard (associated with the Greater London area) and other similar newspapers.
- University/College accommodation lists (available from most Universities/Colleges).
- Other publications, many of which are free and are available in larger cities, carry specialist letting sections.

All these can be picked up at minimal cost.

FACTORS AFFECTING LEVELS OF RENT

Once a rental band has been established the property itself should be looked at in order that market values can be approximated. This tends to be based on opinion and an open mind should be kept at all times. It is often strange that landlords will "hold out" for a specific amount (per week), based on a completely arbitrary figure. In such cases it would be more prudent to accept a lower rent where the contract can start at an earlier date, than to hold out for the "desired" price and run the risk of the property being empty for a week or so. It is therefore sensible to assess each "let" on its own merits, by compromising between all the factors.

Other factors which will affect the rental level of the property can be considered here, these are:-

- The number of bedrooms - the number of bedrooms available in the property often has a much greater effect on price than at first thought. It is very common for a group of individual sharers to want a bedroom each and will often wish to convert a reception room for use as a further bedroom. In extreme cases tenants will convert all available bedrooms and forgo the "luxury" of a communal living room. For example a house which might be advertised for sale as having four bedrooms and two reception rooms may well be advertised for letting as having six bedrooms ! But beware of creating an H.M.O. (see section on planning controls).

- The size of the bedrooms is also something which may well affect the price of a property. Most people prefer to have a good size bedroom (especially if they are forgoing a living room) and thus where a house may have three large bedrooms and one "box" bedroom (common in houses built between 1930 to 1950) it may well prove more difficult to let (or be let at a lower price) than a house with four average size bedrooms.

- The condition of the property is of great importance and is becoming even more important as the amount of property, available in the rental market increases. The state of the decorations is vital as well as the condition of the carpets, furnishings etc. Taste and quality thresholds vary greatly from person to person. Unless you are re-decorating and re-furnishing to a very high standard, it is wise to use plain colours and fabrics. Patterns are usually a matter of individual preference and what is tasteful to one person may be offensive to another. Always stick to plain carpets, curtains and furnishings as they never go out of "fashion" and tenants can then personalise the property with their own possessions.

- The contents of the property can also affect the price but more likely will affect the speed with which it can be let; the most frequently requested "luxuries" are:-
  1. Washing machine - considered essential by those who do not wish to sit in launderettes for hours on end !

2. Shower - usually requested in addition to a bath, but some tenants will require a shower as a necessity.
3. Access to garden - usually for hanging washing out or sun-bathing in the summer. Size not normally important and larger gardens can be a handicap and can become a burden to the tenant. (N.B. where a garden is included make sure that the "agreement" includes a clause regarding responsibility for maintenance).
4. Central heating - many tenants will not even look at properties which are not centrally heated. Gas fire or storage heaters are not usually a satisfactory substitute.
5. The position of the property within the locality can have an effect on the price. Some people prefer to be in quieter residential positions whereas others may wish to be in a highly populated area which is well lit at night.
6. Local amenities which are available for everyone to use are also advantageous when letting, for example the price can be affected if there are shops within close proximity and in built-up areas, car parking is becoming increasingly important.
7. Transport affects different areas of the country in different ways. Within London it is the "tube" which has the greatest affect on price. Buses and trains are also important but to a lesser degree. It seems to be easier to let a poor house which is close to a tube station than a similar house in excellent condition which is not within easy walking distance of the underground.
8. In some areas there are also very marked seasonal variations, with increased demand at peak times. In University towns this may be at a maximum in September, with little or no demand once everyone has "found" a property for the academic year.

CHAPTER 2 - MARKET RENTS

Considering all the above factors is very important when valuing a property. Lettings prices are very much based on the "supply and demand" of the localised economy.

When valuing a property avoid being confused by those factors which most certainly *do not* apply !.

An all to common mistake is for a landlord to assume that the rent should be set at a level which enables him to cover his outgoings (i.e. mortgage, service charges, insurances etc.)

The landlords outgoings will bear no relevance to the rental value, whatsoever !.

CHAPTER 2 - MARKET RENTS

CHAPTER 3 - TYPES OF TENANTS

Every landlord is obviously looking for those perfect tenants who will keep his property in pristine condition, pay the rent on time and not be a nuisance to the neighbours. These may seem very simple requests but as any landlord will know things are not always so straight forward. The one thing that can be said is that no group of tenants is better than any other and human nature is such that any landlord will have a certain amount of problems (as tenants will experience with landlords).

By assessing each group on its own merits it is possible to pick the right tenants for your property.

By picking the right tenants for your property, your future problems will be greatly reduced and the management of the property will be far easier.

Be warned !! It is against the law to discriminate against a group of tenants purely on racial grounds (see section on racial discrimination).

STUDENTS

Students form a large proportion of the private sector housing market; they tend to stay for only 8/9 months of the year, this can mean that the property is empty for 3/4 months, during the summer.

In some areas it is not possible to rent out houses for these months; in other areas it is possible to find summer students willing to take on short tenancies. Care should be taken to use the correct contracts for periods shorter than six months (see section on contracts)

Student tenancies are not without their problems, as students tend to require large houses at relatively low rents. This can mean that houses are at the lower end of the market and are sometimes in poorer condition. This can lead to problems between landlords and tenants over maintenance and /or responsibility for repairs. Care should also be taken to make sure that any tenancy complies with the regulations for Houses in Multiple Occupation, where appropriate. (see section on planning controls).

PROFESSIONALS/WORKERS

Working people are obviously a major proportion of the rental market; these vary from people who will be renting in the private sector for an extended period of time, to those who are moved around the country for short periods, because of their employment.

In some cases these tenants may already be home owners and be unable to sell their property at a "reasonable" price, preferring to let their property and rent one to accommodate their increasing family, or rent one in a different location (often to follow employment re-location).

Society is becoming much more mobile and as a result the private rental sector has become much stronger, particularly at a time when house prices are not increasing at a considerable rate.

The major advantage with tenants from this group is that the rent can be covered by the wages/salary earned. It can also indicate whether the tenant is a responsible member of the community, especially where this employment has been for an extended period with the same employer. The main disadvantage of this category of tenants is that people can be made redundant at any time and then the landlord may find himself at the mercy of the Local Authority for the rent payments (see section on housing benefit claims).

CHAPTER 3 - TYPES OF TENANTS

FAMILIES

As a generalisation families tend to be good tenants due to the responsibility of parenthood. The advantages are that they tend to stay in the same accommodation for longer periods due to them being in a more "stable" period of their lives and the difficulty and problems of children constantly changing schools.

However, the property may be subject to increased "wear and tear" where children are involved.

PRIVATE SECTOR LEASING

There exist many large groups and associations who will lease properties from private individuals on a medium term lease. The normal length of such a lease is around two to three years. It is usual for either Local Authorities or Housing Associations to do this. All Associations/Authorities have their own criteria for renting; the following is an example of the kind of arrangement that may be available. Full information should be obtained from the Association/Authority you are proposing to deal with.

Most Associations/Authorities lease these properties to homeless families within their jurisdiction.

Most private leases are underwritten by a Local Authority, although this may not be the Local Authority where the property is situated. i.e. it is common for one Local Authority to lease a property within the boundaries of another Authority.

This underwriting means that the landlord is guaranteed the rent for the duration of the lease, payable by the Local Authority.

Current demand makes one and two bedroom flats most popular, but this will depend on your locality and may include larger houses.

Properties where a Local Authority has held an interest (ex-council) are not normally dealt with. Some properties over shops may also prove unsatisfactory.

- The Association/Authority will usually offer a competitive rent. This will be paid from the date the lease commences to the date the lease expires, regardless of whether the property is vacant over any period during the lease.
- Some Associations/Authorities will pay rents quarterly in advance. In cases where the tenants do not pay their rent to the Association/Authority, this will not affect the payment to the landlord.
- The landlord will be indemnified against the charges levied on the property for gas, electricity, water, council tax, telephone etc. during the lease. He will, however be responsible for the payment of any service charges, building insurances etc.
- Internal repairs are usually carried out by the Association/Authority. The landlord will normally be responsible for the exterior of the property. Where the landlord refuses to carry out works which are his responsibility, the Association/Authority will carry out the works and deduct the cost from the rent.
- The property will normally be let as a family unit and not to groups of individuals.
- The landlord will be guaranteed vacant possession at the end of the contract. The tenants will be on short term licences which would not offer security of tenure.

- Where the landlord lives in the United Kingdom, tax details will be required. Where the landlord lives abroad, the Association/Authority will have to deduct tax at the basic rate (see section on income tax).
- The Association/Authority will also require:- proof of ownership, copy of current building insurance, sanction of lease by mortgagor (where appropriate).
- The property will usually be surveyed by the Association/Authority and the following installations tested:- plumbing, central heating, electrics.

The following is a list of the type of furnishings usually required.

Kitchen:-
Cupboards and work surfaces.
Electric/gas cooker.
Fridge with freezer.

LOUNGE:-
Three piece suite.
Dining table with four chairs.
Coffee table.
Net curtains.
Curtains.

DOUBLE BEDROOM:-
Double bed.
Large wardrobe.
Chest of drawers.
Bedside table(s) x 2
Net curtains.
Curtains.

SINGLE BEDROOM:-
Single bed.
Wardrobe.

Chest of drawers.
Bedside table.
Net curtains
Curtains.

All rooms will need to have light shades and carpet (vinyl in bathroom and kitchen) Smoke detectors are required in living rooms and halls.

HOUSING BENEFIT CLAIMS

"Housing Benefit" is a social security benefit paid to tenants who have a low income and need help with their rent. This housing benefit is paid through the Local Authority. It can also be called "rent rebate" or "rent allowance".

The rules and regulations are constantly changing and care should be taken to ensure that any potential tenant really is eligible.

A claim is awarded for a specific "benefit period". A new claim will be required at the end of each period.

A person is currently eligible for housing benefit if he has a low income and has rent to pay:-

- The claimant could have a partner or be single.
- The claimant could live alone or with other people.
- The claimant could be a pensioner.
- The claimant could be in or out of work.
- The claimant could be employed or self-employed.
- The claimant does not need to have paid any National Insurance contributions.
- The claimant does not need to be a British Citizen.

The benefit entitlement is means tested. Anyone with less than £3000 in savings will qualify for maximum benefit. Savings between £3000 and £16000 will still qualify for benefit, but this will be reduced at a rate of £1 per week for every £250, over £3000. Anyone who has more than £16000 in investments or savings will not be entitled to housing benefit.

Savings include other capital such as shares and certain property, other than your own home.

Savings of a couple are added together BUT the £3000 to £16000 limits do not double, they remain the same whether you are single or a couple.

The Local Authority works out how much benefit will be paid. The maximum that can be paid is 100 % of the "eligible rent".

The "eligible rent" may not be the same as the rent for the property. The eligible rent may be restricted if the home is either unreasonably large or expensive for the claimant's needs.
The claimant will be asked to fill in a very detailed form in order that the claim can be assessed. To avoid delays the claimant should provide as many details as possible. The form will require:-

- Claimants personal details.
- Type of letting:- i.e. house, flat, number of rooms.
- Position of room:- i.e. ground floor, first floor.
- Number of occupants.
- Repairing obligations etc.

In the case of most new lettings the Local Authority will give the completed form to the Rent Officer who will decide whether the rent demanded, is reasonable.

This will be assessed against a market rent for similar properties, paid by those not claiming benefit. It will also be assessed whether the accommodation is of the appropriate size and cost for the claimant.

CHAPTER 3 - TYPES OF TENANTS

Where the rent demanded is considered too high the "Rent Officer" will carry out a valuation, usually including an inspection of the property. The rent officer's decision will be used for housing benefit purposes.

Where there is a disagreement over the amount of housing benefit given, the council will usually provide a statement, detailing how they have worked the benefit out. The decision can normally bc reviewed by a local review board. Contact the Local Authority for further information.

The tenant will be liable for the full rent agreed with the landlord, regardless of any contribution towards the rent, paid by housing benefit.

To help both landlord and tenant decide whether a particular property is suitable for a particular tenant, it is now possible to have a "Pre-Tenancy Determination", which is carried out by an independent rent officer. The pre-tenancy determination will indicate the maximum amount of rent that may be met by housing benefit, however it does not guarantee that this is the amount of housing benefit that will be paid.

The housing benefit can be paid in one of two ways, either direct to the tenant or direct to the landlord.

A word of warning to the inexperienced landlord !
Where the payments are made direct to the tenant, there is a risk that a dishonest claimant will not pass the money on to the landlord. The risk increases the longer the claim remains unpaid. Waiting times vary from one Local Authority to another, but it has been known for claims to take up to six months to be processed !. Dishonest claimants have allegedly disappeared with the first benefit cheque, which in delayed claims can amount to several thousand pounds !!

Where the payments are made direct to the landlord the above situation cannot arise, however, there can be other problems, particularly where the claimants situation changes, or if the claim itself is fraudulent. The Local Authority may take weeks or even months to find out that a claimant is no longer eligible for benefit and that he should be paying his rent from his earnings. The Local Authority not only has the power to stop the benefit once it has discovered the change in circumstances or fraud, but it also can (and will) claim back the overpayment. This is demanded from the recipient of the cheque NOT the claimant, leaving the landlord to chase the tenant for the balance of the rent. We have recently heard of a Local Authority who has just discovered a fraudulent claim, which has been going on for two years. It is currently in the process of reclaiming over £12,000 from the (innocent) landlord who will have the impossible task of claiming this money from a tenant who has no savings. **You have been warned !**

RACIAL DISCRIMINATION

There now exists a statutory code drawn up by the Commission for Racial Equality called the "Code of Practice in Rented Housing", this code has been approved by Parliament and sets out the law. It is unlawful under the Race Relations Act 1976 to discriminate against anyone on racial grounds; that is because of colour, race, nationality or ethnic origin. The code applies to England, Scotland and Wales and covers all areas of rented housing irrespective of the contract used, by Local Authorities, Housing Associations, Co-operatives, private landlords etc.

Racial discrimination can occur in two main forms:-

- Direct discrimination can occur when someone is treated less favourably than another on racial grounds.

- Indirect discrimination occurs when a requirement or condition is applied, albeit unintentionally, which has a detrimental effect on a particular racial group, unless it is justifiable on non-racial grounds.

Further information can be obtained from:-

The Commission for Racial Equality
Information Section
Elliot House
10-12 Allington Street
London SW1E 5EH
Tel: 0171 828 7022

CHAPTER 4 - SUITABLE TENANTS

Careful consideration by the landlord is required at this stage about whether he is to use an Accommodation/Letting Agency or whether to attempt to let the property himself (see section on Letting Agencies).

One is not necessarily to the exclusion of the other and many landlords will put their properties with agents while also attempting to let them privately.

WHERE DO I ADVERTISE ?

When advertising a property "To Let" it is important to consider the method of advertising in order to attract the right type of tenant for the property. If the property is in good condition and professional people are the desired tenants the advert should be placed in the correct place/newspaper, similarly if students are required then the advert should be placed in the type of publications that students read.

There are many methods of advertising which will cover the whole range of potential tenants.

The local press is a very common source of advertising for both private landlords and agencies. In most areas, these days, there are free local papers aimed specifically at giving the community current information and allowing businesses and services the opportunity to advertise. These papers are usually delivered free to every house in the area and provide a relatively cheap form of advertising to all the local community.

There also exist many specialist newspapers which have sections aimed specifically at the private rental market.

In London and many other areas of the country LOOT is available. This "Free-ad" paper is currently published six times a week and has the advantage

that all adverts from private advertisers are free. The paper is available from newsagents and costs about £1.30. It is read by tenants from across the board and is seen as a major source of accommodation for the private rental sector.
There are other specialist "Ad-papers" similar to LOOT and these are available in many areas of the country.

The local newsagent's window may all prove a good source of tenants, for a very low outlay.

College, Hospitals and other such institutions all have accommodation problems and usually have departments specifically aimed at finding suitable accommodation.

Try contacting the personnel departments of local companies, many larger companies need accommodation for their employees, if they regularly move them around the country.

USING A LETTING AGENT

There are many advantages to using a good "letting agent", but there can be more disadvantages if you use a bad one, apart from the financial implications. With more and more agents opening up every day and no regulatory body to control them, the opportunities for cowboys and conmen are growing.

Letting agents usually provide two main services and although these will change from agency to agency, they can be summarised as follows:-

1. Introduction service, this should include:
- The introduction of suitable tenants.
- The provision and completion of the relevant contract documentation, between the landlord and the tenant.

- The securing and confirmation (where possible) of references. Where a landlord requires specific references this instruction should be made clear to the agent.
- The securing of a deposit and advance rent.

2. Management service, as above, but also including:-

- The creation of an inventory for the property.
- Rent collection.
- Organisation of any property maintenance.
- Day to day problem solving.
- Contact point for tenant to discuss problems.
- Regular inspection of property.

A third service is becoming more popular and some landlords find this advantageous. This is "guaranteed" rent provided by an agency. Under these circumstances the agent will pay the landlord the agreed rent for the contract period, whether this rent is collected or not. Fees are not charged for this service, but the agreed rent is usually paid at a much lower rate than the market rent, in order that the agent can make his money. The rent will also be paid whether the property is occupied, or not.

The landlord will have no control over who the agent puts in the property and this can lead to many complications. Responsibility for the condition of the property should be very specific.

Care should be taken by the landlord to ensure that he trusts the agent as the landlord will be left to "clear up the mess" if the agency goes into liquidation. (a repeated result for some agents). The landlord might even be left with sitting tenants, or a "wrecked" house, if he is not careful.

Different agencies will provide different services for the fees charged and full written details of the service provided are a must for the prudent landlord.

Fees will generally range from 5% to 10% for tenant introduction and from 10% to 15% for full management. These fees will usually be subject to VAT.

Fees are usually based on the total rent for the contract.

Where an introduction service is used, the fee is nearly always charged at the beginning of the contract from the advance rent paid by the tenant.

For a management service it is more likely to be deducted every time the rent is paid by the tenant i.e. monthly, weekly etc.

Where the introduction service is used and the landlord pays the fees "up-front" it is unlikely that the agent will refund any fee where the tenant leaves the property within the contract period. The agent will argue that he has provided the landlord with the means to ensure that the tenant remains at the property for the duration of the contract (i.e. a legally binding, enforceable contract).
In practice, however, most landlords do not pursue their tenants through the courts, due to the high cost of court action. They normally prefer to allow the tenants to leave on an "amicable" basis, cut their losses and re-let the property to new tenants as soon as possible.

Under usual circumstances the agency will only be acting as the landlord's "agent" and therefore the contract will be between the landlord and the tenant. It would commonly be up to the landlord to issue legal proceedings against the tenant through the courts (where this is necessary). The agent will normally be called as a witness to any events, or to verify rent arrears etc.

CHAPTER 4 - SUITABLE TENANTS

As with most things in life there are those who are good at their job and those who are not so good. This seems to be more of a problem with "lettings" as there are no qualifications needed to become an agent and there is no governing body which an agent must join. All membership is voluntary and therefore "cowboys" can roam free !

Be warned ! Find out as much as you can about the individual company you propose to use BEFORE placing your property with them. This is absolutely vital if you require guaranteed rent. Try to get as much of this information as possible in writing, i.e. a list of services with a list of fees.

The following are just some of the questions you should consider asking.

1. What are your fees for:-
- Introduction ?
- Rent collection ?
- Full management ?

2. What does each of these services include and/or exclude ?

3. How are fees charged ?
- In advance for the whole period
- Monthly

4. Does the agency guarantee the rents, if the tenants don't pay ?

5. What if the tenants leave before the original contract expires, will any of the fee be refunded ?

6. Where the tenants stay longer than the original contract, will I be charged again ? And if so at what rate ?

7. What happens to the tenants deposit ?

CHAPTER 4 - SUITABLE TENANTS

There is no official governing body as far as letting agents are concerned, there are however, three main organisations who monitor their members and who would give the landlord (and tenant) the extra security and knowledge that they are dealing with a member of a larger overseeing organisation. The three organisations are NAEA (National Association of Estate Agents), ARLA (Association of Residential Estate Agents) and RICS. (Royal Institution of Chartered Surveyors).

NAEA:
The NAEA was established in 1962 and among other aims it is there to "promote unity and understanding among estate agents and to protect the general public against fraud, misrepresentation and malpractice".

Membership of the association is open to persons practising as estate agents (this includes the sale and letting of land and buildings).

Entry standards are high and are at the discretion of the association council.

There are strict rules of conduct for NAEA members and it has disciplinary and complaints procedures.

The association has a "guarantee bonding scheme".

For further details and a list of members in your area, contact them on:- 01926 496800

ARLA:
The Association of Residential Letting Agents was formed in 1981 as a national professional and regulatory body for member firms working in the field of letting and managing residential property.

CHAPTER 4 - SUITABLE TENANTS

ARLA appraises and regulates all member companies and provides guidelines, training and advice.

ARLA member firms are fully bonded and hold Professional Indemnity Insurance to protect the financial interests of landlords and tenants.

In order for an agency to become a member, the following criteria must be met:

1. The company must be a genuine company being either limited or a partnership. It must have been trading as a letting agency or an estate agency for a minimum of two years.
2. The company must be trading from strictly business premises and not from a home environment.
3. The company must have a current Professional Indemnity Insurance policy.
4. The company must operate separate company and client's bank accounts in order that client's money is kept completely separate.
5. Commission must be obtained only from landlords.

Once ARLA are satisfied that an agency complies with the above, it is invited for an interview with two Council members. The Council members will go into some detail to establish that the agency in question has sufficient knowledge of Housing Legislation and that their "Modus Operandi" is acceptable and up to ARLA standards.

ARLA has grown considerably over the last five years.

ARLA work closely with the Department of the Environment and is recognised by both sides of the House of Commons.

For further information, contact them on: 0171 734 0655.

RICS:
The Royal Institution of Chartered Surveyors is the most prestigious of the three organisations and has very strict entrance examinations, controls and disciplinary procedures.
The RICS has divisions covering every aspect of surveying; property management is only a small part of their "umbrella".

For further information, contact them on: 0171 222 7000

General advice:

Try to deal with an agent who has been recommended to you.

Where this is not possible the best alternative is to use an Agent who is a member of a recognised body.

Beware of the increasing number of "cowboys".

It is illegal for an accommodation agency to charge tenants a fee for merely providing a list/details of properties.
However, it is not illegal (and is common practice in some areas) for an agent to charge a fee where the tenant takes a property. The tenant should be made aware of this at the outset i.e. at the time when he starts looking and not when he comes to sign contracts.

CHAPTER 5 - MAKING APPOINTMENTS

When placing advertisements in newspapers or elsewhere, it is sensible to make sure that you are able to cope with any response generated. There is no point in having potential tenants enquire about viewing the property if no-one is available to show them. It is as well to set aside the following few days after the adverts are published in order that maximum advantage can be made of any response.

When making appointments do not worry about people turning up at the same time to view the property. It is all very well making appointments at half hourly intervals but you will find that it is human nature to bc unreliable and so you may fine that very few of the appointments will be on time; many will not turn up at all, but don't get annoyed ! Just assume that you wouldn't want a tenant who doesn't have the courtesy to cancel an appointment which he no longer requires !

At this stage of the proceedings it is best to see as many potential tenants as possible in order that you get the widest possible choice, don't be put off by those who don't necessarily have a good telephone manner, make appointments to meet them.

When arranging these appointments make it clear which references you will require from your tenants to avoid wasting your and other people's time. Complicated references are not available from everyone and this is best cleared up before you meet your potential tenants.

Have a list of basic questions ready, close to the telephone. But ! do not go "over the top" as many people will be put off by an over nosy landlord. Striking a balance is difficult but very important. The ideal landlord is one that is interested enough to be concerned about his property, but will allow the tenants "quiet enjoyment" of the property without undue interruptions. Tenants do not like the kind of busy-body landlord who has nothing better to do than interfere all the time.

If you are arranging for people to go direct to the property, then try to get there early in order that you may make it as inviting as possible. This can be easily done by turning on the heating and have the place properly lit. Tenants will be put off by a cold, untidy, musty, dimly lit property; even though it may have great potential.

When showing the property encourage the potential tenants to ask as many questions as they want. It is important that any potential problems are aired at this stage in order that they can be sorted out.

Clearly explain the payment arrangements, covering the following:-

- How much the rent is per period.
- What the period is (i.e. per week, per four weeks, per calendar month etc. - see glossary of terms for an explanation).
- Whether the rent is to be paid in advance.
- How payments are to be made.
- What deposit is required.

Answer all questions with definite answers, as vague promises will lead to future problems. Where for example, the tenants ask for you to provide/remove any furniture then answer with a “yes” or a “no” - do answer with comments like “I’ll see what I can do” - this is a potential disaster area. It is when communication breaks down that things start to go wrong and problems occur.

When discussing the different aspects of the property be vary careful not to talk about things over which you have no control.

CHAPTER 5 - MAKING APPOINTMENTS

Where the services are to be connected in the tenant's own name, make them aware of this. In some circumstances there may be a large deposit that the relevant authority will ask them to pay. This will depend entirely on their own personal circumstances and is not something on which the landlord should comment. Do not promise the tenants that a telephone line is available. This is something that the tenants must sort out for themselves. Do not comment on the availability of a line, but comments like "The previous tenants had a telephone" are better, as it may be that the line has been removed since the previous tenants vacated. This is something over which you will have no control.

CHAPTER 5 - MAKING APPOINTMENTS

CHAPTER 6 - PREPARING THE PROPERTY

FURNISHED OR UNFURNISHED ?

Historical Housing Laws have created a difference between the rental of a furnished and an unfurnished property. The rights of the landlord and those of the tenant were completely different where premises were let under these conditions. Tenants found it easier to prove a sitting tenancy where the property was unfurnished. This distinction does not apply where an Assured Shorthold Tenancy is used. (see section on contracts).

As a consequence of these now outdated laws there is a much larger proportion of furnished accommodation to that of unfurnished, on the private rental market.

The decision whether to rent out on a furnished or unfurnished basis will depend entirely on the individual landlord's own circumstances. The type of tenants required will be the main factor. In general, those renting a furnished property will tend to stay for a shorter period compared with those renting unfurnished property. This is obviously due to the physical problems of moving the furniture from one property to another. Students and those of a transient nature will be attracted to furnished properties as they are less likely to have furniture of their own.

REMEMBER !
That any furniture provided by the landlord will have to comply all relevant regulations. Unfurnished properties will (obviously) not have to comply with these furniture regulations ! (see section on the Furniture and Furnishings (Fire)(Safety) Regulations 1998 + amendments)

CHAPTER 6 - PREPARING THE PROPERTY

FURNISHED PROPERTIES

Where a property is let as "fully furnished" the landlord should provide everything for the tenants to live up to the standard of that property. If, for example, the property is of a very high standard and in an exclusive area, then the furniture and equipment should also be of a high standard. The higher the quality of the property, the higher the quality of equipment expected.

INVENTORY

An important part of preparing a property, is to draw up a full inventory of all the landlord's possessions within the property, stating the condition and make of the appliances etc. Time spent at this point will avoid all sorts of misunderstandings, when the tenants come to move out.

Sample inventory

Property: 41 Accommodation Ave
Landlord: Mr Reasonable
Tenant: Mr Reliable
Date prepared: 1.2.1997

ITEM	BRIEF DESCRIPTION	CONDITION
Living room:		
Carpet	Brown patterned	Fair (2 x stains)
Settee	Beige striped	Good
Chairs x 2	Ditto	Ditto
Table	Wooden	Excellent - no scratches

Signed (landlord)..
Signed (tenant)...

CHAPTER 6 - PREPARING THE PROPERTY

APPLIANCES

All appliances should be serviced and checked before the tenants take occupation of the property, to ensure that they are in good, safe, working condition. The tenants should be given any relevant instruction manuals in order that they are able to work the appliances correctly, particularly items such as boilers and washing machines. The tenancy agreement should also contain specific clauses relating to the servicing and/or repair of this type of item, in order to avoid confusion where appliances malfunction. All gas appliances will have to be maintained in accordance with the Gas Safety (Installation and Use) Regulation 1988. The tenants should always notify the landlord/managing agent of any problems as and when they occur.

CHAPTER 6 - PREPARING THE PROPERTY

CHAPTER 7 - CHOOSING TENANTS

Having seen as many potential tenants as possible it should be fairly obvious which of those are seriously interested. If you are unsure who is interested then ask them. Those who give vague answers are probably not interested, so discount them.

Where, for example you have three groups who seem interested, then concentrate on these.

The main objective at this time is to obtain as much information as possible about all the individuals concerned. It is at this juncture that the tenants will be the most forthcoming, in order to secure the property for themselves.

Always make sure that any information given by the tenants is verified. Where any information provided cannot be verified before the tenants move in, discount it. Once the contracts have been signed the tenants will have the security that they require and the references will have served their purpose in persuading you to sign the contract document. From this moment on, it is the conditions of the contract which will be of the greatest importance.

REFERENCES

When obtaining references always remember that they can be falsified. Try to confirm written references with their author. It's often not the references themselves that are important, but that by asking for them you can usually tell how forthcoming the tenant has been. A tenants who had hoped to "bluff" his way into your property, will soon go for an easier "target" when he sees that written references really will be required.

Most tenants can obtain references within a few days, if they really want to. Where the tenant insists that they will take longer (perhaps after the date when they wants to move in), then be slightly suspicious.

In the case where time is not a major consideration then it is best for the landlord to apply for the references himself. Some employers will not release references unless written requests are received.

Where time is an important factor it is usually quicker for the tenants to organise the references and for the landlord to verify them by telephone.

Remember ! references are only there to give an indication of the likely behaviour of the tenant and a landlord will usually have no "comeback" on the reference provider.

Work reference

It is important for any potential tenants to provide a work reference, if they are in employment. The reference should be on headed paper and be written by someone in a position of trust. The reference should include as much information as possible, for example:-

- Nature of employment (permanent/temporary)
- Length of time employed.
- Approximate salary.

Landlord's reference

Another very important source of information on a potential tenant. A landlord's reference should be confirmed by telephone, wherever possible, as it is always helpful to speak to their previous landlord direct, in order to find out how suitable you think the proposed tenant would be. The reference should include:-

- Address of property
- Length of time resident at this address.
- Amount of rent being paid.
- Whether rent was regularly paid on time.

- Condition of property.
- Other aspects, such as, if they were noisy etc.

It should be noted that some landlords will provide bad tenants with good references in order that they can get rid of them from their property. Speaking to the landlord in person will usually indicate if there has been a problem.

Character reference

These can be obtained by most people (whether employed or not). For this type of reference to be of any use they should be written by someone who is an upstanding member of the community, for example:- Doctor, Bank Manager etc.

Like the other references they should be verified and should ideally contain.

- Relationship with the tenant.
- Period that the tenant has been known.
- General attitude towards other people's property.
- Whether reliable and trustworthy etc.

Bank reference

Ironically, these are probably the references that most landlord's seek and are probably the most vague and therefore of least use.

They take a reasonable time to come through, they cost between £8 and £25 (plus VAT) per reference and they are vague in their descriptions.

It is quicker and easier to ask to see the tenants previous (three?) bank statements as this will give you a better idea of the financial stability of the tenant.

The following is a useful list of information you may wish to ask the tenant for, before contracts are signed:-

- Name.
- Date of birth.
- Current address and telephone number.
- Employer's name, address and telephone number.

- College's name, address and course being attended (for students)
- Parents name, address and telephone number (for students only?)
- Current landlord's name, address and telephone number.

Remember ! Once you have installed a tenant the only way to remove them is via the Courts, which can be a long expensive process.

Before signing and letting the tenants move in, be extremely careful !

- Thoroughly check all references.
- Make sure you are 100% happy.

Don't be persuaded to take on someone you are uncertain about ! It may be tempting if they are offering you some rent/deposit now, but you will have to chase them for all future payments, if they become unreliable!.

CHAPTER 8 - CONTRACTS GENERALLY

The contract is the most important part of letting a property. Without it you will not part with ownership of the property but it is possible to part with possession of the property indefinitely, in that the tenants may have security of tenure and this will mean you will be unable to get vacant possession of the property, should you need it for any reason (i.e. to sell it). In practical terms the value of the property will be greatly reduced if a tenant has security of tenure.

It is for this reason that we strongly recommend that you consult a solicitor before you let out a property, to ensure that you understand the implications.

One such solicitor has edited the following chapters and he can be contacted as follows:-

Mr Richard Jones
Bury and Walkers
4 Butts Court
Leeds LS1 5JS
Tel: 0113 244 4227
Fax: 0113 246 5965

Bury and Walkers provide a comprehensive service for landlords (and their agents), which includes:

- Preparation of tenancy agreements.
- Provision of all tenancy documentation.
- Advice in respect of rent arrears, breaches of tenancy agreement etc.
- Possession proceedings.
- Planning aspects of letting.
- Environmental Health considerations.
- Houses in Multiple Occupation (H.M.O.s).
- Advice and assistance on all aspects of the Landlord and Tenant relationship.

CHAPTER 8 - CONTRACTS GENERALLY

Under no circumstances should you enter into a contract unless you are aware of exactly what you are doing.

Fully completed Assured Shorthold tenancy agreements can be purchased by "next day" mail order (see section on mail-order contracts) and we strongly recommend that this service or a solicitor is used to draw up your agreements. Filling in blank forms is a disaster area to those who are not trained to do so.

There follows a brief explanation of the most likely contractual arrangements for the private landlord. This is not intended to be a full explanation of the 1988 Housing Act, nor an authoritative view on contractual arrangements, but is here to indicate the types and styles of available contracts.

Where a landlord is considering letting out part or all of a property it is vital that he is aware that, unless the correct contract is used (and the chosen contract is used correctly), he may well be giving the tenant long term rights to that property; the tenant may have a statutory right to remain.

HOUSING ACT 1988

The Government has made a conscious effort to increase the private sector rental market and, in order to do this, has made it possible to enter into a contract where the tenant has no on-going security of tenure. Specifically it is the Housing Act of 1988 that has made this possible, where contracts were entered into, on or after 15th January 1989. This Act enables an Assured Shorthold Tenancy to be granted where an Assured Tenancy can be created.

It is usually the Assured Shorthold Tenancy which is of greatest interest to the private landlord. As will be seen in the following chapters there are additional requirements for entering into an Assured Shorthold tenancy, but the tenancy must also be an Assured Tenancy.

Assured Tenancies can only be created in certain circumstances and a brief summary of these situations are listed below:-

- A complete self-contained dwelling - i.e. House etc. - In this case an Assured Tenancy can be created under Part 1 section 1 of the 1988 Housing Act.
- A dwelling which is not self-contained but where the tenants do not have to share facilities, only access corridors etc. In this case an Assured Tenancy can be created under Part 1 section 1 of the 1988 Housing Act.
- A room or bedsit where only the bathroom or WC is shared with other tenants. - In this case an Assured Tenancy can be created under Part 1 section 1 of the 1988 Housing Act.
- A room or bedsit where any living accommodation is shared with others. In this case an Assured Tenancy can be created under Part 1 section 3 of the 1988 Housing Act.

Under the Housing Act 1988 living accommodation includes a lounge, dining room, bedroom or kitchen, but excludes bathroom or WC

It is important to note that an Assured Tenancy cannot be created in the following situations:

- A room or bedsit where living accommodation is shared with the landlord.
- Business premises.

The legislation regarding business premises is not dealt with in this guide.

One specific type of Assured Tenancy is an Assured Shorthold Tenancy (AST). Some of the rules, especially those relating to how the landlord recovers possession of his property, are different for Assured Shorthold Tenancies. These are explained separately.

For the purpose of this guide, and to make the explanation clearer, it has been assumed that all tenancies have been created on or after 15th January 1989 and that they are with new tenants and not tenants who have existing rights under earlier legislation.

Part 1 section 1 of the 1988 Housing Act covers those situations in which Assured Tenancies can be created.

The Act contains the following wording:-

"A tenancy under which a dwelling-house is let as a separate dwelling is....an assured tenancy...."

"A dwelling-house" means:-

- House.
- Part of a House.
- Flat.
- Maisonette.
- Bedsit etc.

"Which is let" means:-

- That a tenancy must be created, not merely a licence to occupy e.g. a lodger. Those who are required to occupy the premises as part of their job are excluded, i.e. caretakers etc.

"A separate dwelling" means:-

- Accommodation that is a single unit where the tenant can carry out the normal activities of living i.e. sleeping, cooking, relaxing, and eating without sharing. Where the tenant has to share bathroom facilities or a WC an assured Tenancy can still be created.

CHAPTER 8 - CONTRACTS GENERALLY

An Assured Tenancy can still exist where the tenant shares living accommodation in certain circumstances.

SHARING FACILITIES

Part 1 section 3 of the 1988 Housing Act covers the situation where the tenant shares his living accommodation with other tenants. As long as the tenant has exclusive use of some part of the accommodation, for example a bedroom, he is able to be an assured Tenant with the right to use the shared accommodation. Where the tenant shares the living accommodation with the landlord, an Assured Tenancy cannot be created. (see section on letting a room in your home).

COMPANY LETS

A tenancy can only be an Assured Tenancy if the tenant is an individual. Where there is a joint tenancy the joint tenants must all be individuals. Companies are not able to be Assured Tenants. Thus the company has no right to remain once the tenancy has ended. However a court order will be needed to enable the landlord to regain possession if anyone is still residing in the premises.

BOARD

Under the 1988 Housing Act an Assured Tenant will still be an Assured Tenant even if the landlord provides board.

Likewise there can still be an Assured Tenancy where services are provided. However, if the landlord provides a service which requires him to have unrestricted access to and use of the premises, the occupier could well be a lodger and not a tenant.

LANDLORD'S ADDRESS FOR SERVICE OF NOTICES

Every landlord MUST notify the tenant of an address where the tenant can serve notices on the landlord. Failure to do so means that no rent is legally due from the tenant until the landlord has complied with his requirement. The address must be an address in England or Wales. It need not be the landlord's home address, instead it can be the address of the managing agent. There is no prescribed form of notice. One way of complying with this requirement is to include a clause in the contract. Notification must be in writing. The suggested form of wording is:-

"The landlord hereby notifies the tenant pursuant to section 48 of the Landlord and Tenant Act 1987 that the address at which notices (including notices in proceedings) may be served on the landlord is:

[insert address in England or Wales]"

If a landlord does not observe this obligation he may get a nasty shock when he sues for any arrears of rent because they will not be lawfully recoverable until notification is given. However, failure to give the notice does not mean that any rent that is payable before the notice is given is lost for all time.

CHAPTER 9 - ASSURED TENANCIES

The basic criteria are summarised as follows:-

- It is the form of tenancy for most new residential lettings, unless validly created as an Assured Shorthold Tenancy.
- The property must be let as a separate dwelling or the tenant must have exclusive use of at least one room which is living accommodation.
- It must be the tenant's only or main home.
- It may be written or oral.
- Terms will be agreed prior to commencement.
- The tenant will have long term security of tenure, unless it is an Assured Shorthold Tenancy.
- If the tenancy is an Assured Tenancy rather than an Assured Shorthold Tenancy, the tenant does not have to leave unless he wishes to go, or the landlord has grounds for regaining possession, which he can prove in court.
- The tenant cannot apply to the rent officer for a fair rent, but will pay the rent agreed with the landlord.

LENGTH OF TENANCY

When the tenancy is granted it can either be for a fixed period of months/years (a fixed term tenancy) or it can be for an indefinite period (a contractual periodic tenancy). The interval at which the rent is paid to the landlord will decide the length of the period, i.e. weekly, monthly, etc.

When the fixed term comes to an end the parties may agree to create another fixed term tenancy or a periodic tenancy (a contractual periodic tenancy). If there is no such agreement then the tenancy will automatically become a statutory periodic tenancy; this is a new tenancy imposed on the parties by the Housing Act 1988. The terms will be the same as under the fixed term tenancy which has ended (including the rent). The only difference is that it is now a periodic tenancy. The periods of the tenancy (i.e. weekly, monthly, etc.) will be decided by the intervals at which the rent was last paid to the landlord under the expired fixed term tenancy.

RENT CHANGES

Where the tenancy is a fixed term tenancy, the agreement will usually provide for changes to the rent. This will often state that it will go up by a certain amount on a certain date or it may be linked to the Retail Prices Index. Otherwise it cannot be altered during the fixed term unless both the landlord and the tenant agree to the alteration. Once the fixed term has ended and another fixed term is agreed, a new rental level can be agreed.

Where the tenancy is a contractual periodic tenancy, unless the parties can agree the new rent or the tenancy provides for making an increase, the landlord will have to increase the rent within the formal procedures of the Housing Act 1988, unless the landlord and the tenant can agree the new rent. Increases under this procedure are only permitted once per year. When a statutory periodic tenancy starts after a fixed term has run out the procedure can be implemented as soon as the statutory tenancy comes into existence and at yearly intervals from that date.

If there is a provision within the agreement that provides how and when the rent is to be altered the parties are unable to apply to the Rent Assessment Committee.

Where there are no provisions within the agreement for the rent to be altered the landlord must propose the increase on the prescribed form. He must give the tenant the appropriate notice as follows:-

- Periodic tenancy of one month or less - notice of at least one month.
- Periodic tenancy of one to six months - notice of one period.
- Periodic tenancy of exceeding six months - notice of six months.

The notice must specify that it takes effect on the first day of a rental period.

Where the tenants agrees with the increase in rent, he will start paying the increased rent from the date the notice runs out.

The parties can come to some mutual agreement regarding the new level of rent.

Otherwise, where the tenant disagrees with the level of rent proposed, he must apply to the Rent Assessment Committee for their decision (See Rent Assessment Committee), before the landlord's notice expires. Afterwards it is too late. If the notice is referred to the Committee it does not take effect until after the Committee has made its decision. However, unless the Committee decide otherwise, the increase will be backdated to the date specified in the landlord's notice as the date on which the increase was to take effect.

RENT ASSESSMENT COMMITTEE

The Rent Assessment Committee is a body of independent people from various backgrounds. Some of them will have relevant technical backgrounds i.e. Surveyors, Solicitors etc. And some of them will have no relevant technical background i.e. laymen.

The Committee is appointed by the Lord Chancellor and the Secretary of State for the Environment.

CHAPTER 9 - ASSURED TENANCIES

These Committees have been in existence for some time, setting Fair Rents under the Rent Act 1977.

The Committee will be chosen from a panel of appointed people. There are 14 such panels in England and Wales. Normally three members sit to hear cases.

The committee will make its decision from studying the relevant papers, but either the tenant or the landlord can request a hearing which both may attend. This hearing would be informal and there is no charge for the Committee's services.

The application to the Rent Assessment Committee must be on the prescribed form.

The Committee will decide the rent level the landlord can reasonably expect if he were to let the property on the open market, with a new tenancy which:-

- would be of the same period as the current one, (e.g. weekly or a monthly tenancy).
- would start from the date when the proposed increase was to take effect.
- would have the same terms as the current tenancy.

The Committee will not take into account:-

- the fact that the tenant may be a sitting tenant within the premises and what effect this may have on the rent.
- any improvements to the premises carried out by the current or, in certain circumstances, an earlier tenant, except those which are carried out as a condition of the tenancy agreement.
- any reduction in the value caused by the tenant, from a failure to look after the property under the terms of the agreement.
- any variable service charges.
- any council tax.

There is no appeal against the Rent Assessment Committee's decision, except on a point of law.

Neither the landlord nor the tenant can ask for the rent officer to set a rent.

The Rent Assessment Committee has the power to change the terms of the agreement. This is a similar process to a change in the rent.

GROUNDS FOR POSSESSION

When a landlord wants his property back from an Assured Tenant he has to serve notice on the tenant saying that he wants the property back and that he intends to go to court. This notice is given under Part 1 section 8 of Housing Act 1988. When this notice is served he has to state which one of the "grounds for possession", provided by the Act, he is using. This notice must be on the prescribed form and be for a period of either two weeks for some grounds and two months notice for other grounds. The notice must set out the full text of the ground(s) relied on. It must also give particulars of the ground(s). For example if there are rent arrears it must state the amount of the arrears and the date to which they are calculated.

There are two types of grounds set out in the Act:-

- Mandatory - The court MUST grant possession of the property to the landlord if he proves one of these grounds.
- Discretionary - The court MAY grant possession of the property to the landlord if he proves one of these grounds. Whether the court will grant possession will depend whether it thinks it is reasonable to do so.

Some of the grounds are "prior notice" grounds. These can only be used if the landlord informed the tenant, in writing, BEFORE the contract commenced, that he intended to use one of them. In some instances, however, the court might grant him possession if it thought there were good reasons for the notice not being served.

The following is a summary of those grounds which may be relevant to the private landlord.

GROUND 1
(Mandatory, prior notice except at court's discretion, possession notice period of two months). Where the landlord used to live in the property as his only or main home, or he intends to move into it as his only or main home.
This ground cannot be used:-
- where the landlord (or an earlier landlord) bought the property after the tenancy had commenced.

This ground can be used:-
- where there are joint landlords and only one lived in the property,
- where the landlord's husband or wife intends to live in the property.

(see section on owner occupiers for more information on Ground 1)

GROUND 2
(Mandatory, prior notice except at court's discretion, possession notice of two months). Where the property is subject to a mortgage granted before the tenancy commenced and the mortgagee, often a Bank or a Building Society, wants to sell it, usually to pay back mortgage arrears.

GROUND 3
(Mandatory, prior notice, possession notice of two weeks). Where the tenancy is for a fixed term not exceeding eight months and at some time within the previous twelve months before the tenancy was granted, the property was let or licensed for a holiday.

GROUND 4
Not relevant to the private landlord.

GROUND 5
Not relevant to the private landlord.

GROUND 6
(Mandatory, possession notice of two months). Where the landlord intends to redevelop the property, or a substantial part of it, and cannot do so with the tenant in occupation.
This ground cannot be used:-
- where the landlord bought the property after a sitting tenancy had commenced.
- where the landlord can do the work around the tenant.

GROUND 7
(Mandatory, possession notice of two months) where a periodic tenant has died and proceedings are started within twelve months of this death.
This ground cannot be used:-
- where someone has a statutory right to succeed to the tenancy.

This ground can be used:-
- where the proceedings are started within twelve months of the date where, in the court's opinion, the landlord knew of the tenant's death.

GROUND 8
(Mandatory, possession notice of two weeks). Where the rent is at least three months overdue when the landlord served the notice for possession and is at least three months overdue at the date of the hearing.

GROUND 9
(Discretionary, possession notice of two months). Where suitable alternative accommodation is available for the tenant or will be when the order for possession takes effect.

GROUND 10
(Discretionary, possession notice of two weeks).
Where the tenant was behind with the rent when the landlord served notice that he wanted the tenant to leave and the rent was still in arrears when he began court proceedings.

GROUND 11
(Discretionary, possession notice of two weeks).
Where the tenant has been persistently in arrears with the rent, even if the rent was not in arrears when he began court proceedings.

GROUND 12
(Discretionary, possession notice of two weeks).
Where any of the obligations under the tenancy have been broken or not performed, other than one relating to the payment of rent.

GROUND 13
(Discretionary, possession notice of two weeks).
Where the condition of the property has deteriorated due to the adverse behaviour of the tenant or his guests.

GROUND 14
(Discretionary, possession notice of two weeks).
Where the tenant or his guests have been guilty of conduct which is a nuisance or annoyance to the neighbours. Where the tenant or his guests have been convicted of using the property, or allowing it to be used, for illegal or immoral purposes.

GROUND 15
(Discretionary, possession notice of two weeks).
Where the condition of the furniture provided has deteriorated due to the adverse behaviour of the tenant or his guests.

CHAPTER 9 - ASSURED TENANCIES

GROUND 16
(Discretionary, possession notice of two months).
Where the tenancy was granted because the tenant was employed by the landlord, or a previous landlord, and is no longer employed by him.

 Form No. 3 of the Assured Tenancies and Agricultural Occupancies (Forms) Regulations 1988.

HOUSING ACT 1988

Section 8

Notice of Seeking Possession of a Property Let on an Assured Tenancy

- Please write clearly in black ink.
- Do not use this form if possession is sought from an assured shorthold tenant under section 21 of the Housing Act 1988 or if the property is occupied under an assured agricultural occupancy.
- **This notice is the first step towards requiring you to give up possession of your home. You should read it very carefully.**
- If you need advice about this notice, and what you should do about it, take it as quickly as possible to any of the following—
  - a Citizens' Advice Bureau,
  - a Housing Aid Centre,
  - a Law Centre,
  - or a Solicitor.

  You may be able to get Legal Aid but this will depend on your personal circumstances.

(1) Name(s) of tenant(s).

1. To([1]):

(2) Address of premises.

2. Your landlord intends to apply to the court for an order requiring you to give up possession of([2]):

- If you have an assured tenancy under the Housing Act 1988, which is not an assured shorthold tenancy, you can only be required to leave your home if your landlord gets an order for possession from the court on one of the grounds which are set out in Schedule 2 to the Act.
- If you are willing to give up possession of your home without a court order, you should tell the person who signed this notice as soon as possible and say when you can leave.

(3) Give the full text of each ground which is being relied on. (Continue on a separate sheet if necessary).

3. The landlord intends to seek possession on ground(s) ______ in Schedule 2 of the Housing Act 1988, which reads([3]):

- Whichever grounds are set out in paragraph 3 the court may allow any of the other grounds to be added at a later date. If this is done, you will be told about it so you can discuss the additional grounds at the court hearing as well as the grounds set out in paragraph 3.

[P.T.O.

Notice Seeking Possession, Section 8 (side 1)

(4) Give a full explanation of why each ground is being relied on. (Continue on a separate sheet if necessary).

4. Particulars of each ground are as follows([4]):

- If the court is satisfied that any of grounds 1 to 8 is established it must make an order (but see below in respect of fixed term tenancies).
- Before the court will grant an order on any of grounds 9 to 16, it must be satisfied that it is reasonable to require you to leave. This means that, if one of these grounds is set out in paragraph 3, you will be able to suggest to the court that it is not reasonable that you should have to leave, even if you accept that the ground applies.
- The court will not make an order under grounds 1, 3 to 7, 9 or 16, to take effect during the fixed term of the tenancy; and it will only make an order during the fixed term on grounds 2, 8 or 10 to 15 if the terms of the tenancy make provision for it to be brought to an end on any of these grounds.
- Where the court makes an order for possession solely on grounds 6 or 9, your landlord must pay your reasonable removal expenses.

(5) Give the date after which court proceedings can be brought.

5. The court proceedings will not begin until after([5]):

19

- Where the landlord or licensor is seeking possession under grounds 1, 2, 5 to 7, 9 or 16 in Schedule 2, court proceedings cannot begin earlier than 2 months from the date this notice is served on you and not before the date on which the tenancy (had it not been assured) could have been brought to an end by a notice to quit served at the same time as this notice.
- Where the landlord is seeking possession on grounds 3, 4, 8 or 10 to 15, court proceedings cannot begin until 2 weeks after the date this notice is served.
- After the date shown in paragraph 5, court proceedings may be begun at once but not later than 12 months from the date this notice is served. After this time the notice will lapse and a new notice must be served before possession can be sought.

To be signed by the landlord or his or her agent (someone acting for him/her).

Signed:	
Name(s) of landlord(s):	
Address of landlord(s):	

If signed by agent, name and address of agent

Telephone:		Date:	19

HA 32

4 94 F27013
5045277
* *

Notice Requiring Possession, Section 8 (side 2)

CHAPTER 9 - ASSURED TENANCIES

CHAPTER 10 - ASSURED SHORTHOLD TENANCIES.

An Assured Shorthold Tenancy is a type of Assured Tenancy.

The most important feature of an Assured Shorthold Tenancy is that the landlord has a guaranteed right of possession once the fixed term comes to end. It is favoured by most landlords because of this.

The basic criteria of an Assured Shorthold Tenancy are:-

- Guaranteed right of landlord to re-possess his property at the end of the tenancy.
- The term must be for a minimum fixed period of six months. It can be for longer, but it is inadvisable to grant an Assured Shorthold Tenancy for more than a year.
- The tenant has security of tenure throughout the fixed term, although if there are rent arrears or if the tenant breaks the terms of the tenancy the landlord can apply to the Courts for possession.
- There must be no right for the landlord to break the fixed term during the first six months, unless the tenant fails to pay or is otherwise in breach.
- The landlord must serve notice of the tenancy on the prescribed form (see section notice of Assured Shorthold Tenancy).
- An Assured Shorthold Tenancy cannot be granted by a landlord to a tenant of his, who is already an Assured Tenant.
- An Assured Shorthold Tenancy can be granted by a landlord to a tenant of his who is already an Assured Shorthold Tenant.
- The terms of the Assured Shorthold Tenancy can be freely agreed between the landlord and the tenant. There are, however, certain circumstances where the tenant can refer the rent to the Rent Assessment Committee.

An Assured Shorthold Tenancy involves three documents, all of which are extremely important to

CHAPTER 10 - ASSURED SHORTHOLD TENANCIES.

the whole contract. Care should be taken when drawing up the contract, in order to ensure its validity.

- Notice of an Assured Shorthold Tenancy.
- Agreement.
- Notice requiring possession.

A Housing Bill was published on 18 January 1996 and at the time of publication is currently making its way through Parliament and so is not law yet. The proposed changes include amendments to the requirement for notices of tenancy described below, but until this has become law, the following is still in force.

NOTICE OF TENANCY

This is served on the tenant once the basic details of the tenancy have been agreed and before the parties sign the tenancy agreement. The function of this form is to notify the tenant that they will be taking part in an Assured Shorthold Tenancy Agreement.

A copy of this notice appears on the following pages and the form contains the following information:-

a) The name(s) of proposed tenant(s).
b) The address of the property.
c) The start date of contract.
d) The end date of contract (minimum six months after start date).
e) The name of landlord.
f) The address of landlord.
g) The telephone number of landlord.
h) The signature of landlord (or an agent if acting on his behalf)
i) The name of agent (if applicable)
j) The address of agent (if applicable)
k) The telephone number of agent (if applicable)
l) The date of notice.

CHAPTER 10 - ASSURED SHORTHOLD TENANCIES.

Where a joint tenancy of a property is to be granted to more than one tenant, one notice naming all of the tenants should be given.

The notice must be given to the tenants to retain, it must not just be shown to them.

Notifying the tenants in this way gives them the opportunity of taking the form to their own Solicitor or the Citizen's Advice Bureau and thus they are able to gain independent advice on the implications of the contract.

This form MUST be served on the tenants BEFORE the tenancy agreement is entered into, otherwise the tenants will be Assured Tenants who have long term security of tenure.

The landlord should keep a copy of the notice. It is prudent for the landlord to obtain the tenant's signature confirming receipt, in order that it could be proved at any time in the future that the tenant had notice of the contract - copies of all documents should obviously be retained.

This form should be served on the tenant prior to the signing of the contract in order that the tenant has enough opportunity to decide to obtain independent advice. The time period is not prescribed, but the tenant must be given at least sufficient time to read the notice through properly.

If the commencement date or the termination date are altered after the notice has been given, then a new notice containing the revised dates should be served before the tenancy agreement is entered into.

It is vital that details on this notice are the same as under the agreement i.e. names of landlord and tenant, length of tenancy and the address of the property to be let.

CHAPTER 10 - ASSURED SHORTHOLD TENANCIES.

 Form No. 7 of the Assured Tenancies and Agricultural Occupancies (Forms) Regulations 1988 (as amended)

HOUSING ACT 1988

Section 20

Notice of an Assured Shorthold Tenancy

- Please write clearly in black ink.
- If there is anything you do not understand you should get advice from a solicitor or a Citizens' Advice Bureau, before you agree to the tenancy.
- The landlord must give this notice to the tenant before an assured shorthold tenancy is granted. It does not commit the tenant to take the tenancy.
- **THIS DOCUMENT IS IMPORTANT, KEEP IT IN A SAFE PLACE.**

(1) Name of proposed tenant. If a joint tenancy is being offered enter the names of the joint tenant(s).

To([1]):

1. You are proposing to take a tenancy of the dwelling known as:

(2) The tenancy must be for a term certain of at least six months.

([2]) from the day of 19
to the day of 19

2. This notice is to tell you that your tenancy is to be an *assured shorthold tenancy*. Provided you keep to the terms of the tenancy, you are entitled to remain in the dwelling for at least the first six months of the fixed period agreed at the start of the tenancy. At the end of this period, depending on the terms of the tenancy, the landlord may have the right to repossession if he/she wants.

3. The rent for this tenancy is the rent we have agreed. However, you have the right to apply to a rent assessment committee for a determinaton of the rent which the committee considers might reasonably be obtained under the tenancy. If the committee considers (i) that there is a sufficient number of similar properties in the locality let on assured tenancies and that (ii) the rent we have agreed is significantly higher than the rent which might reasonably be obtained having regard to the level of rents for other assured tenancies in the locality, it will determine a rent for the tenancy. That rent will be the legal maximum you can be required to pay from the date the committee directs. If the rent includes a payment for council tax, the rent determined by the committee will be inclusive of council tax.

[P.T.O.

Notice of Assured Shorthold Tenancy (side 1)

CHAPTER 10 - ASSURED SHORTHOLD TENANCIES.

To be signed by the landlord or his/her agent (someone acting for him/her). If there are joint landlords each must sign, unless one signs on behalf of the rest with their agreement.

Signed:

Name(s) of landlord(s):

Address of landlord(s):

Telephone:

If signed by agent, name and address of agent

Telephone:

Date: 19

SPECIAL NOTE FOR EXISTING TENANTS

- Generally, if you already have a protected or statutory tenancy and you give it up to take a new tenancy in the same or other accommodation owned by the same landlord, that tenancy cannot be an assured tenancy. It can still be a protected tenancy.
- But if you currently occupy a dwelling which was let to you as a protected shorthold tenant, special rules apply.
- If you have an assured tenancy which is not a shorthold under the Housing Act 1988, you cannot be offered an assured shorthold tenancy of the same or other accommodation by the same landlord.

1993 Edition
5.95 F29579
5045316
* *

HA 35

Notice of Assured Shorthold Tenancy (side 2)

CHAPTER 10 - ASSURED SHORTHOLD TENANCIES.

AGREEMENT

The agreement is the main part of the contract and is the basis on which the property is let. It will contain all the relevant clauses which both the tenant and the landlord have to abide by.

The landlord and the tenant are generally free to agree the clauses between them.

The agreement will contain the following information, which, where applicable, must match with the notice:-

a) The date of contract.
b) The name of the landlord.
c) The name of the tenant.
d) The address of the property.
e) The term of the contract (in months or years), (N.B. this must be for a minimum fixed period of six months - it must not be backdated).
f) The contract commencement date.
g) The amount of the rent.
h) The rental period.
i) The rental payment period.
j) The payment day.
k) The date of first payment.
l) The obligations of the tenant.
m) The obligations of the landlord.
n) The signature of the landlord
o) A witness to the signature of the landlord.
p) The signature of the tenant.
q) A witness to the signature of the tenant.

The landlord and tenant must agree the clauses and obligations of the contract at this stage. These clauses should include all the express stipulations that either party requires.

CHAPTER 10 - ASSURED SHORTHOLD TENANCIES.

Any limitations either party require on the tenancy should also be included, for example, no pets or no children.

One party cannot unilaterally alter the contract afterwards, so it is vital to ensure that any provision which is required is included at the outset.

The tenancy agreement should contain a clause (commonly called a forfeiture clause enabling the landlord to terminate the fixed term early when the tenant does not pay the rent on time or otherwise is in breach of the tenancy agreement). Such a clause should not allow for early termination for any other reason.

Where an agreement says that the landlord can re-enter the property if there is a breach by the tenant it is vital that this is not read literally. Despite the wording a landlord must apply to the Court for possession if anyone (at all) is residing at the property.

Clauses which contradict the essence of the contract should not be included, such as a variation in the notice periods etc., as this may render the contract void. Thus there must be no right for the landlord to terminate the tenancy during the first six months, except where the tenant is in arrears with his rent or has broken the terms of the tenancy. However, where both parties want it, the tenant can be given the right of early termination (for example one month's notice) even during the minimum fixed term of six months.

Where any subject is not included within the contract and a problem occurs, references will be made to any relevant statute such as the 1988 Housing Act, or common law. The general obligations of the landlord and the tenant under the 1988 Housing Act are described later.

CHAPTER 10 - ASSURED SHORTHOLD TENANCIES.

The landlord should obtain a standard form of contract from a law stationer such as "The Law Stationers Society Ltd" (Oyez), have the agreement drawn up by a Solicitor, or have it completed by mail order.

MAIL-ORDER CONTRACT SERVICE

Take the worry out of preparing your own agreements.

Alpha-Lets (UK) Ltd on 0181 800 4313, provide a mail order service which sends out "fully completed Assured Shorthold Tenancy Agreements" by first class post.

The process is very simple; just telephone them when you have agreed all the tenancy details and they will send out (first class) the agreements which should arrive the next day.

All the landlord and tenant need to do is sign the agreements !!

Two copies of the contracts are provided (one for the landlord and one for the tenant).

The bound agreements contain six pages of clauses to cover most eventualities and will greatly assist the landlord in the management of the property.

All the relevant notices are included.

This service is covered by their Professional Indemnity Insurance.

The total cost of this service including VAT, Postage and Packaging is only £19.96.

CHAPTER 10 - ASSURED SHORTHOLD TENANCIES.

AGREEMENT

for letting furnished dwellinghouse on an assured shorthold tenancy under Part I of the Housing Act 1988

> **This is a form of legal document and is not produced or drafted for use, without technical assistance, by persons unfamiliar with the law of landlord and tenant.**
>
> **Note that the notice condition in the Housing Act 1988, s.20(1)(c), requires prior service of notice in the prescribed form.**
>
> **This form should not be used for granting a tenancy to a person who is already a protected or statutory tenant or a protected occupier: see Housing Act 1988.**

DATE 19

PARTIES 1. **THE** Landlord

2. **THE** Tenant

PROPERTY The dwelling-house situated at and being

Together with the Fixtures Furniture and Effects therein and more particularly specified in the Inventory thereof signed by the parties

*The number of months must not be less than six: Housing Act 1988, s.20(1)(a).

†The period mentioned here will form the basis of any subsequent periodic tenancy

TERM A term certain of *months/year(s) from 19

RENT £ per †(subject nevertheless as hereinafter provided)

PAYABLE in advance by equal payments on

First payment to be made on the day of next

1. **THE** Landlord lets and the Tenant takes the Property for the Term at the Rent payable as above

2. **THIS** Agreement is intended to create an assured shorthold tenancy as defined in section 20 of the Housing Act 1988 and the provisions for the recovery of possession by the Landlord in section 21 thereof apply accordingly

Agreement of an Assured Shorthold Tenancy (side 1)

tax. This is still the case where you have a lodger who is treated as a member of the family. Where you let part or all of your house, you may be liable for some capital gains tax. This will depend on the amount of your home which has been let and the length of time for which it has been let out.

Where part or all of your property has been used as your home at any time, you may qualify for a special exemption.

FURNISHED HOLIDAY LETTINGS

It may be possible to let your property as holiday accommodation, thereby obtaining the valuable tax benefits of carrying on a trade; these benefits include a wider allowability of expenses, rollover relief and retirement relief.

There are certain strict conditions which must be met before your property can qualify for this treatment and professional advice MUST be sought from your accountant BEFORE attempting to let your property in this manner.

RESIDENCE

Income tax is ALWAYS payable on rent received, after allowable expenses, if a property in the UK is let, EVEN where the landlord is defined as not being resident for tax purposes.

From 6th April 1996, a new scheme came into effect which applies to both the rental income and other income of a UK rental business due to a landlord whose usual place of abode is outside the United Kingdom, where the rent is paid on or after that date. In such a case the letting agent (or tenant where no agent has been appointed) must deduct tax at the appropriate rates, from the landlord's UK rent received (less allowable expenses) on a quarterly basis. However, the non-resident landlord can apply to the Inland Revenue's Financial Intermediaries and

- Building insurance premiums.
- Water rates, council tax (if appropriate), ground rents.
- Costs of maintaining gardens, communal areas, roads, drains etc., where the landlord is responsible.
- Interest on a Bank or Building Society loan made to purchase or improve the rented property.
- The cost of "wear and tear" of furniture can be dealt with in one of two ways. EITHER a "wear and tear" allowance of 10% of the annual rent (after deducting council tax, water rates and any other service charges) can be applied OR the actual cost of furniture as and when it is replaced. Once an option has been chosen, it cannot be changed.

A proportion of any of the above costs is allowable where only a part of the dwelling is let.

MORTGAGE INTEREST RELIEF AT SOURCE (MIRAS)
Providing less than one third of your property is let, then tax relief through the MIRAS scheme should not normally be affected. However, if you rent more than one third, the Inland Revenue will instruct your lender to collect your mortgage interest without the relief. Relief will then be available as an allowable expense, described above.

Should you rent your entire property and take out a second loan to purchase a further property as your home, tax relief will be available on the interest charged on both loans. Firstly, through MIRAS on the loan to purchase your new home and secondly, on the initial loan on the now rented property, treating that interest as an allowable expense.

CAPITAL GAINS TAX
Where you have a house which is your only or main residence you are not usually liable for capital gains

3. **WHERE** the context admits—

(*a*) "The Landlord" includes the persons for the time being entitled in reversion expectant on the tenancy

(*b*) "The Tenant" includes the persons deriving title under the Tenant

(*c*) References to the Property include references to any part or parts of the Property and to the Fixtures Furniture and Effects or any of them

4. **THE** Tenant will—

(*a*) Pay the Rent at the times and in the manner specified

(*b*) Pay for all gas electricity and water consumed on or supplied to the Property during the tenancy and the amount of all charges made for the use of the telephone (if any) at the Property during the tenancy or a proper proportion of the sums demanded for the aforesaid utilities and facilities to be assessed according to the duration of the tenancy (for the avoidance of doubt such payment will be due in relation to amounts attributable to standing charges annual rates or levies or the like and to VAT as well as to actual consumption)

(*c*) Not damage or injure the Property or make any alteration in or addition to it

(*d*) Preserve the Fixtures Furniture and Effects from being destroyed or damaged and not remove any of them from the Property

(*e*) Yield up the Property at the end of the tenancy in the same clean state and condition as it was in the beginning of the tenancy and make good pay for the repair of or replace all such items of the Fixtures Furniture and Effects as shall be broken lost damaged or destroyed during the tenancy (reasonable wear and damage by fire excepted)

(*f*) Leave the Furniture and Effects at the end of the tenancy in the rooms or places in which they were at the beginning of the tenancy

(*g*) Pay for the washing (including ironing or pressing) of all linen and for the washing and cleaning (including ironing and pressing) of all counterpanes blankets and curtains which shall have been soiled during the tenancy (the reasonable use thereof nevertheless to be allowed for)

(*h*) Permit the Landlord or the Landlord's agents at reasonable hours in the daytime to enter the Property to view the state and condition thereof

(*i*) Not to assign sublet or otherwise part with possession of the Property without the prior written consent of the Landlord but so that it is hereby agreed for the purposes of section 19A of the Landlord and Tenant Act 1927 that if the Landlord consents to an assignment of the Property such consent may be given subject to the condition that the Tenant will enter into an authorised guarantee agreement within the meaning of the Landlord and Tenant (Covenants) Act 1995

(*j*) Not carry on on the Property any profession trade or business or let apartments or receive paying guests on the Property or place or exhibit any notice board or notice on the Property or use the Property for any other purpose than that of a strictly private residence

(*k*) Not do or suffer to be done on the Property anything which may be or become a nuisance or annoyance to the Landlord or the Tenants or occupiers of any adjoining premises or which may vitiate any insurance of the Property against fire or otherwise or increase the ordinary premium for such insurance

(*l*) Permit the Landlord or the Landlord's agents at reasonable hours in the daytime within the last twenty-eight days of the tenancy to enter and view the Property with prospective Tenants

(*m*) Perform and observe any obligation on the part of the Tenant arising under the Local Government Finance Act 1992 or regulations made thereunder to pay council tax and indemnify the Landlord against any such obligation which the Landlord may incur during the tenancy by reason of the Tenant's ceasing to be resident in the Property

Agreement of an Assured Shorthold Tenancy (side 2)

5. **PROVIDED** that if the Rent or any instalment or part thereof shall be in arrear for at least fourteen days after the same shall have become due (whether legally demanded or not) or if there shall be a breach of any of the agreements by the Tenant the Landlord may re-enter on the Property (subject always to any statutory restrictions on his power so to do) and immediately thereupon the tenancy shall absolutely determine without prejudice to the other rights and remedies of the Landlord

6. **THE** Landlord agrees with the Tenant as follows—

(1) To pay and indemnify the Tenant against all assessments and outgoings in respect of the Property (except any council tax and any charges for the supply of gas, electricity and water or the use of any telephone payable by the Tenant under clause 4 above)

(2) That the Tenant paying the Rent and performing the agreements on the part of the Tenant may quietly possess and enjoy the Property during the tenancy without any lawful interruption from the Landlord or any person claiming under or in trust for the Landlord

(3) To return to the Tenant any rent payable for any period while the Property is rendered uninhabitable by fire the amount in case of dispute to be settled by arbitration

7. **THIS** Agreement shall take effect subject to the provisions of section 11 of the Landlord and Tenant Act 1985 if applicable to the tenancy

8. **NOTICE** under section 48 of the Landlord and Tenant Act 1987

The Tenant is hereby notified that notices (including notices in proceedings) must be served on the Landlord by the Tenant at the following address‡:

‡This must be an address in England and Wales

AS WITNESS the hands of the parties hereto the day and year first above written

SIGNED by the above-named (the Landlord)

in the presence of

SIGNED by the above-named (the Tenant)

in the presence of

Agreement of an Assured Shorthold Tenancy (side 3)

CHAPTER 10 - ASSURED SHORTHOLD TENANCIES.

DATED 19

and

AGREEMENT

for letting furnished dwellinghouse at

on assured shorthold tenancy

Rent £

 Agreement 20

Agreement of an Assured Shorthold Tenancy (side 4)

CHAPTER 10 - ASSURED SHORTHOLD TENANCIES.

NOTICE REQUIRING POSSESSION

The third document is the notice requiring possession. This should be served by the landlord on the tenants at least two months before he wishes the contract to end. This form officially notifies the tenants that the contract is to be terminated and that the landlord requires the property back on a specific date.

The contract cannot be terminated within the fixed period using this notice; however, if the tenant defaults, possession can still be claimed during the fixed term (see section on grounds for possession). If, for example, the contract is for a minimum period of six months and the landlord requires the property back at the end of that six month period, then the notice should be served at least two months before the end of the contract. (i.e. before the end of the fourth month).

Where this notice has not been served the tenants are entitled to stay on at the property and the agreement can continue indefinitely; the tenancy will still be an Assured Shorthold Tenancy.

When the fixed term expires and unless a new tenancy has been agreed, a statutory periodic tenancy will arise if the tenants remain in the property (see section on Assured Tenancies).

Even where a statutory periodic tenancy has arisen the landlord has the flexibility to serve the minimum two months notice, but the rules are different.

The notices are different depending on whether they are given to the tenants during the fixed term or after the fixed term has expired.

CHAPTER 10 - ASSURED SHORTHOLD TENANCIES.

It is the time when the notice is received by the tenant which is crucial in deciding which type of notice is given, not the date when the tenancy is to be terminated.

Both notices contain the following information:-

a) The name of the tenant.
b) The address of the tenant.
c) The name of the landlord.
d) The address of the landlord.
e) The address of the property.
f) The date the tenancy is to be terminated.
g) The date the notice was served.
h) The signature of the landlord.
i) The name of the agent (if applicable)
j) The address of the agent (if applicable)

The notice given during the fixed term and the notice to be served after the fixed term has run out, are both reproduced on the following pages.

CHAPTER 10 - ASSURED SHORTHOLD TENANCIES.

HOUSING ACT 1988

Section 21(1)(b)

Assured Shorthold Tenancy : Notice Requiring Possession:

Fixed Term Tenancy

(Notes)

(1) Name and address of tenant.

To(1)

of

(2) Name and address of landlord (Note 2 overleaf)

From(2)

of

(3) Address of dwelling

I give you notice that I require possession of the dwelling house known as(3)

(4) Date of expiry (Note 3 overleaf)

after(4)

(5) Note 3 overleaf

Dated(5) 19

Landlord

(6) Name and address

[Landlord's agent](6)

[P.T.O.

Notice Requiring Possession - Fixed term (side 1)

CHAPTER 10 - ASSURED SHORTHOLD TENANCIES.

NOTES

1. On or after the coming to an end of a fixed term assured shorthold tenancy, a court must make an order for possession if the landlord has given a notice in this form.

2. Where there are joint landlords, at least one of them must give this notice.

3. The length of the notice must be at least two months and the notice may be given before or on the day on which the fixed term comes to an end.

11.94 F28220

5045201

* * * *

HA 21

Notice Requiring Possession - Fixed term (side 2)

CHAPTER 10 - ASSURED SHORTHOLD TENANCIES.

HOUSING ACT 1988

Section 21(4)(a)

Assured Shorthold Tenancy : Notice Requiring Possession: Periodic Tenancy

(Notes)

(1) Name and address of tenant

To(1)

of

(2) Name and address of landlord (Note 2 overleaf)

From(2)

of

(3) Address of dwelling

I give you notice that I require possession of the dwelling house known as(3)

(4) Date of expiry (Note 3 overleaf)

after(4)

(5) Note 3 overleaf

Dated(5) 19

Landlord

(6) Name and address

[Landlord's agent](6)

Notice Requiring Possession - Periodic Tenancy (side 1) [P.T.O.

CHAPTER 10 - ASSURED SHORTHOLD TENANCIES.

NOTES

1. Where an assured shorthold tenancy has become a periodic tenancy, a court must make an order for possession if the landlord has given proper notice in this form.

2. Where there are joint landlords, at least one of them must give this notice.

3. This notice must expire:

   (a) on the last day of a period of the tenancy.

   (b) at least two months after this notice is given.

   (c) no sooner than the earliest day on which the tenancy could ordinarily be brought to an end by a notice to quit given by the landlord on the same day.

HA 21A

Notice Requiring Possession - Periodic Tenancy (side 2)

CHAPTER 10 - ASSURED SHORTHOLD TENANCIES.

There is no statutory prescribed form of Notice Requiring Possession.

The notice given before the fixed term has run out is given under Section 21(1)(b) of the 1988 Housing Act. Where this notice is served, the date for the termination of the tenancy can be any date at least 2 months after the giving of the notice, but it must be no earlier that the last day of the fixed term.

However, where the Notice Requiring Possession is not given until after the fixed term has run out, Section 21(4) of the 1988 Housing Act applies. The notice must then specifically state the "possession is required by virtue of Section 21 of the Housing Act 1998". The rules for fixing the date when the tenancy is to end are also more complicated. The overriding rule is that at least two month's notice must be given. The date to be specified as the termination date must be the last day of a rental period. If any other date is stated then the notice will be ineffective.

<u>For example:</u>

- An Assured Shorthold Tenancy commenced on 21st May 1995 for six months.
- No notice was given during the fixed term.
- The fixed terms ran out on 20th November 1995.
- The tenant stayed on so a statutory periodic tenancy came into existence.
- As the rent was payable on the 21st of each month, this is a monthly tenancy.
- The last day of each period is therefore the 20th day of each month.
- During January 1996 the Landlord decided that he wanted possession of the property.
- He therefore had to give notice relying on Section 21(4).
- He gave notice on 27th January 1996.

- The date specified in the notice should be 20th April 1996.
- The notice is dated for the end of a period and it was at least two months from when it was served.

Complications occur where the periods of the tenancy are in excess of two months e.g. quarterly, six monthly, or yearly. In such a situation the minimum period of two months is extended to at least one period of the tenancy. It must still run out at the end of a rental period.

RENEWING AN ASSURED SHORTHOLD TENANCY

Where an Assured Shorthold Tenancy is renewed (provided certain conditions are met) the new "identical" tenancy will automatically be an Assured Shorthold Tenancy. This will be so even though the renewed tenancy is for less than six months and even though the prescribed form of notice of an Assured Shorthold Tenancy (Section 20) has not been given. This applies where the landlord, the premises and the tenant are identical under both the old and the new tenancy. These rules apply to any statutory periodic tenancy which arises when the fixed term has run out and the tenant remains in the property. "Identical" means that exactly the same names and the address of the property appear on the old and new agreements. However, for example, if the old tenants were Mr Jones and Mrs Smith, and the new tenancy is only with Mr Jones, this rule would not apply. Wherever there is any change the new tenancy must comply with all the rules for a new Assured Shorthold Tenancy. In particular, it must then be for a minimum fixed term of six months and a notice of Assured Shorthold Tenancy (Section 20) must be given.

CHAPTER 10 - ASSURED SHORTHOLD TENANCIES.

GROUNDS FOR POSSESSION

Where a landlord wishes to regain possession within the fixed term of the contract he can rely on certain of the grounds previously explained (see section on Assured Tenancies), without waiting for the fixed term to run out. However, he can only do so when the tenant is at fault. Grounds 8, 10, 11 or 12 can be used in order to make a claim for possession. Before doing so, notice must be given under Section 8 of the Housing Act 1988 (see section on Assured Tenancies).

Where the landlord wishes to regain possession outside the fixed term he does not have to rely on one of the grounds explained under the section on Assured Tenancies, but can give the tenant the Notice Requiring Possession (see section on Notice Requiring Possession) and rely on Section 21 of the Housing Act 1988.

If the tenant fails to vacate the property after the notice (referred to above) has run out, the landlord must apply for a Court Order. The Court must make on order in such a case.

RENT ASSESSMENT COMMITTEE

During the initial fixed term of an Assured Shorthold Tenancy, the tenant has the right to refer the rent to the Rent Assessment Committee, if it is "significantly in excess" of the market rent for comparable properties. Although there is no rigid rule this probably means that the rent payable by the tenant is more than 10% above "the going rate" for the particular property. The Committee can then make a determination limiting the rent to a market rent. The landlord cannot charge more.

CHAPTER 11 - LETTING A ROOM IN YOUR HOME

Unlike the other chapters the legislation is different where accommodation is let out in a property in which the landlord resides. As with other chapters we are only dealing with new lettings to new tenants which have taken place on or after 15th January 1989.

A resident landlord will have the right to get his property back from his tenant once the contract has been brought to an end. The landlord may need to obtain a Court Order to enable him to do this, if the tenant refuses to go, although this will not always be necessary - see below.

In order to be a resident landlord the letting must fall into one of a number of categories. Firstly, the landlord may share living accommodation with the tenant (for the meaning of "living accommodation" see section on contracts generally). Secondly, if the landlord lets out part of a building but lives in another part of the same building, so long as the building in question is not a purpose built block of flats. Thirdly, the landlord may let out part of a flat and live in another part of the same flat. For either the second or third category to apply the landlord must occupy another part of the building or the flat (as the case may be) as his only or principal home when the tenancy is first granted, thereafter throughout the tenancy and when the tenancy comes to an end, although there are certain exceptions to this rule.

Where the letting falls within any of these categories the tenant will not be an Assured Tenant. Instead the letting will be governed by the terms of the contract. When this comes to an end the normal rule is that a Court Order will be required, to obtain possession if anyone is resident at the property.

CHAPTER 11 - LETTING A ROOM IN YOUR HOME

A Court Order would not be necessary if it is the landlord's only or main home and he shares accommodation in it with the tenant. The property must be the landlord's only or main home when the tenancy was granted and when it ends.

Similarly, a Court Order will also be unnecessary if the tenant shares accommodation with a member of the landlord's family. Both the landlord and the member of his family, must have been living in the property as his only or main home when the tenancy was granted and when it ends. However, for this provision to apply the building must not be a purpose built block of flats.

In deciding whether a Court Order is needed it does not matter that the accommodation is not living accommodation (for the meaning of "living accommodation" see section on contracts generally). However, where there are common entrances, corridors, staircases and storage these do not count as the sharing of accommodation.

Where, under these circumstances, the landlord wishes the tenant to vacate the premises he needs only to serve a simple notice to quit. This notice should be for the length provided for within the agreement and does not need to be on a prescribed form.

Where the tenant refuses to leave even though the landlord does not require a Court Order, then a Solicitor or the Citizen's Advice Bureau should be consulted. In any case although the tenancy may have ended, even though you can evict without a court order, you must not do so if there is anyone actually in the property at the time.

It is advisable for any restrictions on the tenancy to be agreed at the outset and put in writing, in order to avoid any problems in the future.

CHAPTER 12 - OWNER OCCUPIERS

Specific provision is made to enable an owner/occupier to let his property and then get possession back as of right, once the tenancy has ended. The tenant will not then acquire long term rights to the property. As with other topics we are only concerned with new lettings to new tenants from 15th January 1989 onwards. The relevant provision is found in Ground 1 Schedule 2 to the 1988 Housing Act (see section on Assured Tenancies). The tenant will still be an Assured Tenant.

So long as the required notice has been given by the landlord to the tenant before the tenancy began then the landlord is entitled to a Court Order for possession where the landlord has previously occupied the property. The landlord must, however, have lived in the property, before the letting, on the basis that it was his only or principal home at the time. It does not then matter why the landlord requires the property back after the tenancy has finished. The landlord can obtain possession for any reason, including a wish to sell the property.

Alternatively, again provided the required notice has been given at the outset, a landlord who has not lived in the property before the letting can also obtain a possession order but only if he (or his spouse) intends to occupy the property as his (or his spouse's) only or principal home. This provision is intended to cover houses bought to move into later e.g. after retirement. It cannot be relied upon if the tenant was a sitting tenant at the time the landlord bought the property.

In both cases written notice must have been given to the tenants before the beginning of the letting that possession can be recovered under Ground 1. The notice must be given no later than the day on which the tenancy begins. There is no prescribed form of notice (unlike an Assured Shorthold Tenancy) but the notice must make it clear to the tenant that a Court must make an order for possession in these circumstances. The notice can be incorporated in the tenancy agreement itself. This form of notice is reproduced on the following pages.

If you are proposing to let out your home, so long as you have lived in it as your only or main home, you should consider relying on Ground 1 as the tenancy can be either a fixed term tenancy or a periodic tenancy, such as a monthly tenancy. If it is granted for a fixed term it can be shorter than six months and it can contain a break-clause so that the landlord can terminate it early. For example if a landlord has a job abroad he could let his own home for a year but include a break-clause so that should he have to return to this country early then possession can be obtained. There is no right for the tenant to refer the initial rent to the Rent Assessment Committee, unlike in the case of an Assured Shorthold Tenancy.

A prospective owner/occupier, that is someone who has not actually lived in the property, should not rely on Ground 1. When the time comes it may be impossible to demonstrate the necessary intention to occupy the property. Instead the landlord may well wish to sell the property. An Assured Shorthold Tenancy is a preferable option in this situation.

A landlord seeking to recover possession under Ground 1 must give a minimum of two months notice under Section 8 of the 1988 Act. If the tenant fails to vacate, an application to the Court for possession will have to be made, but so long as the conditions for Ground 1 apply, the Court must make an order for possession. There is even a power for the Court to dispense with the required notice if it is just and equitable to do so, but do not rely upon this. Instead make sure that the required notice is given before the tenancy begins.

CHAPTER 12 - OWNER OCCUPIERS

It is vital to remember that in the first place it is the length of the tenancy as granted by the contract which is all important. If you let your own home for a year with no provision for early termination then you cannot get it back early, unless the tenant agrees, however much you may need it.

HOUSING ACT 1988

Schedule 2, Ground 1

Notice of Occupation as Home : Recovery of Possession of Dwellinghouse Let on Assured Tenancy
(Notes)

(1) Name and address of tenant.

To(1)

of

(2) Name and address of landlord.

I(2)

of

(3) Address of dwelling.

give you notice that the possession of the dwellinghouse known as(3)

may be recovered on ground 1 in Schedule 2 to the Housing Act 1988

(4) Note 3 overleaf.

Dated(4) 19

Signed

Landlord

(5) Name and address.

[Landlord's agent](5)

[P.T.O

Notice of Occupation as Home (side 1)

NOTES

1. A landlord of a dwelling let on an assured tenancy will by serving notice in this form recover possession if either:

   (a) before the tenancy, he occupied the dwelling as his only or principal home; or

   (b) he needs it as his or his spouse's only or principal home and (if he is a successor to the original landlord) no person who, as landlord or joint landlord, acquired the reversion since this notice acquired it for money or money's worth.

2. Where there are joint landlords seeking possession, at least one of them must have occupied the dwelling as his home or need it as a home.

3. This notice must be given on or before the day on which the tenancy is entered into (Sched. 2 Part IV para. 11).

4. The court may dispense with the requirement of the notice if it considers it just and equitable.

HA 22

Notice of Occupation as Home (side 2)

CHAPTER 12 - OWNER OCCUPIERS

CHAPTER 13 - HOLIDAY ACCOMMODATION

HOLIDAY LETTINGS

If a landlord lets a property for a holiday, this is not an Assured Tenancy and therefore the 1988 Housing Act will not apply. The letting must genuinely be for holiday purposes. Once the contract has come to an end there is no need to obtain a Court Order for possession. If the tenant fails to vacate you should take advice from your Solicitor or the Citizen's Advice Bureau. In any case even though the tenancy may have come to an end, although you can evict without a Court Order, you must not do so if there is anyone actually in the property at the time.

OUT OF SEASON/WINTER LETS OF HOLIDAY ACCOMMODATION

Special provision is made by the 1988 Housing Act for out of season/winter lets of holiday accommodation. This is dealt with by Ground 3 in Schedule 2 of the Act. It applies so long as the property has been let out for a holiday within the previous 12 months before the out of season let begins. The holiday occupation need not even have been under a tenancy; the holidaymaker may only have a licence. The occupation for holiday purposes must have been by someone other than the landlord.

To qualify under Ground 3 the out of season etc. letting must be under a fixed term tenancy for no more than 8 months. It can be for a shorter period. It must not be a periodic tenancy. A written notice must have been given to the tenant before the beginning of the tenancy that Ground 3 can be relied upon. There is no prescribed form. However, you can purchase forms from Law Stationers such as Oyez (see section on recommended help).

The tenant is an Assured Tenant. When the fixed term has come to an end the Court must then make an order for possession. Before any claim can be made for possession, notice must be given to the tenant under Section 8 of the Housing Act, but only a minimum of 14 days notice is required. If the tenant will not move out once the notice has run out, the landlord can only evict the tenant by obtaining a Court Order.

A letting relying upon Ground 3 has the advantage that, although it must be for a fixed term, there is no minimum period, such as the minimum period of six months required for an Assured Shorthold Tenancy. Further, the tenant has no right to refer the rent to the Rent Assessment Committee.

This provision is therefore very useful to those who live in holiday areas, who wish to let their properties between holiday lets. There can be tax advantages to landlords who let out holiday accommodation and these can extend to the rent received from out of season lettings. They also enable the landlord to know that as and when he wishes to let again for holiday purposes, possession can be obtained.

CHAPTER 14 - LETTINGS FOR UNDER SIX MONTHS.

Many prospective landlord are aware of the requirement that an Assured Shorthold Tenancy has to be for a minimum of six months. Some ask if there is any way that a property can be let out for less than this period, as they may want it back earlier. The short answer is "no", that is unless the letting can be brought within one of a number of categories.

The first possibility is where the letting is by an owner/occupier (see section on owner occupiers). An Assured Tenancy can be granted in reliance upon Ground 1 and thus can be either a periodic tenancy such as a weekly or monthly tenancy or for a fixed term which can be less than 6 months. However, two months notice will always be required in order to obtain possession.

Resident landlords (see section on letting a room in your home) can grant tenancies for less than six months since tenancies granted by them will not be Assured Tenancies at all.

Out of season lettings of holiday accommodation (see section on holiday accommodation) must be for a fixed term but this can be for anything up to eight months. It can therefore be for as short as a month. Furthermore only 14 days notice is required before seeking possession.

A letting to a Company is not an Assured Shorthold Tenancy at all, so again there is no minimum period required.

Unless you can bring yourself within one of these categories, however, you should let by way of the grant of an Assured Shorthold Tenancy, which must, of course, be for at least six months. You can, however, include a break clause under which the tenant can give notice to go earlier. But be warned ! you should never include a break clause in an

CHAPTER 14 - LETTINGS FOR UNDER SIX MONTHS.

Assured Shorthold Tenancy which enables the landlord to terminate early within the first six months (other than where there is a breach of the tenancy terms, or for non payment of rent).

CHAPTER 15 - STANDARD FORMS OF CONTRACT.

Standard forms of contract are available from various sources and come in different formats.

The standard forms highlighted within this guide are reproduced by kind permission of the Solicitors' Law Stationery Society Ltd (Oyez).

For a complete list of forms available from them, contact Oyez Stationery Group, at their head office which is:-

Oyez House
Third Avenue
Denbigh West Industrial estate
Bletchley
Milton Keynes
MK1 1TG

They have various Offices, Retail Shops, etc. Throughout the country.
Telephone 01908 371111 for further details.

The following is a list of forms of most likely use to the readers of this guide and are all available from Oyez.

AGREEMENT FOR LETTINGS - The use of these forms is likely to give notice to an Assured Tenancy under which the tenant will have long term security of tenure.

- Agreement for Letting (General Form)
- Agreement for Letting House
- Agreement Letting Unfurnished Dwellinghouse (Housing Act 1961)
- Agreement for Letting Furnished House or Flat for Holiday
- Agreement for Letting Furnished Flat or Apartments
- Agreement for Letting Flat - Unfurnished

CHAPTER 15 - STANDARD FORMS OF CONTRACT.

- Agreement for Letting Flat - Furnished
- Agreement for Letting Unfurnished Premises to a Tenant Company

ASSURED SHORTHOLD TENANCY (HOUSING ACT 1988)

- Agreement for Letting an Unfurnished Dwellinghouse on an Assured Shorthold Tenancy
- Agreement for Letting a Furnished Dwellinghouse on an Assured Shorthold Tenancy
- Notice of an Assured Shorthold Tenancy (s20)
- Assured Shorthold Tenancy: Notice Requiring Possession: Fixed Term Tenancy (s21(1)(b))
- Assured Shorthold Tenancy: Notice Requiring Possession: Periodic Tenancy (s21(4)(a))
- Application to Rent Assessment Committee for a Determination of a Rent under an Assured Shorthold Tenancy (s22(1))

ASSURED TENANCIES (HOUSING ACT 1988)

- Assured Shorthold Tenancy: Notice that new Tenancy is NOT to be Assured Shorthold (s20(5)) - this is for use when an Assured Shorthold Tenancy is renewed but the landlord wishes to convert the tenancy to an Assured Tenancy. The result will then be that the tenant enjoys long term security of tenure.
- Notice Proposing Different Terms for Statutory Periodic Tenancy (s6(2))
- Application referring a Notice under Section 6(2) to a Rent Assessment Committee (s6(3))
- Notice seeking Possession of a Property Let on an Assured Tenancy (s8) - this notice is given as a preliminary to seeking possession from an Assured Tenant (except where the landlord is claiming possession from an Assured Shorthold Tenant following the expiry of the fixed term of the tenancy).

CHAPTER 15 - STANDARD FORMS OF CONTRACT.

- Landlord's Notice Proposing a New Rent under an Assured Periodic Tenancy or Agricultural Occupancy (s13(2))
- Application Referring a Notice Proposing a New Rent under an Assured Periodic Tenancy or Agricultural Occupancy to a Rent Assessment Committee (s13(4)

RECOVERY OF POSSESSION (HOUSING ACT 1988)

- Notice of Occupation as Home: Recovery of Possession of Dwellinghouse Let under Assured Tenancy (Schedule 2, Ground 1) - this form is used if an owner occupier (or intending owner occupier) is letting a property. It must be given before the tenancy starts.
  Notice of Holiday Accommodation: Recovery of Possession of Dwellinghouse Let on Assured Tenancy (Schedule 2, Ground 3) - this form is used before entering into an out of season/winter let of holiday accommodation. It must be given before the tenancy starts.
- Notice of Student Letting: Recovery of Possession of Dwellinghouse Let on Assured Tenancy (Schedule 2, Ground 4)
- Notice of Requirement for Minister of Religion: Recovery of Possession of Dwellinghouse Let on Assured Tenancy (Schedule 2, Ground 5)
- Notice of Mortgage: Recovery of Possession of Dwellinghouse Let on Assured Tenancy (Schedule 2, Ground 2) - this form should only be used if notice is served under Section 2, Ground 1 at the same time.

NOTICE TO QUIT

- Notice to Quit by Landlord of Premises Let as a Dwelling (Notices to Quit(Prescribed Information) Regulations 1988) - this form will only apply to terminate a periodic tenancy granted to a company or which was an Assured Tenancy but has ceased to be one (e.g. because it is no longer the tenant's only or main home). It must expire on a rent payment day or the day before. The length of notice is equivalent to the period of the tenancy but subject to a minimum of 4 weeks.

CHAPTER 16 - COURT ORDERS.

The purpose of using a contract is to create a legally binding agreement which can be enforced by either party, should the other break one of the clauses (e.g. by failing to pay rent).

It is usual to enforce the contract through the Courts by obtaining the Court's judgement in your favour and thus a Court Order is necessary. This is generally done with the aid of a Solicitor, who will advise you on the likely costs of such action.

This kind of action will not be cheap and should not be undertaken lightly. The probable costs should be weighed against the probable outcome.

Remember ! that although a court may find in your favour, this judgement may not be easy to enforce unless the current whereabouts of the tenants are known.

The tenant may have no money or assets to meet the judgement.

There is no absolute necessity to go to a Solicitor, although in the case of contracts where property is involved, it is always advisable.

Should you decide not to use a Solicitor the local County Court will advise you on how to proceed when applying for Court time.

It should be remembered that applying for Court time is one thing but representing yourself in Court is another. The case may be dismissed if it is not presented correctly.

The strong advice therefore is to consult a Solicitor, in order that time and money are not wasted.

CHAPTER 16 - COURT ORDERS.

The Citizen's Advice Bureau or a Consumer Advice Centre will help.

The County Court will advise you on which forms are required to be completed for your particular circumstances.

They also produce a series of free leaflets which may be of some assistance.

Where the Court finds in your favour any costs in connection with Court fees are usually added to the judgement, as may be some of your Solicitor's fees. Interest on any moneys owed, may also be awarded under some circumstances.

The wait for Court time varies considerably, but it can easily be a number of months.

ACCELERATED POSSESSION CLAIMS

On 1 November 1993, new County Court rules came into force to enable possession claims to be dealt with more quickly. These accelerated possession claims can only be used for Assured Shorthold Tenancies or Assured Tenancies, where possession is sought on Grounds 1 or 3 (and certain other grounds which do not apply to the private landlord).

The following applies:-

- The relevant agreement must have been set up and terminated correctly, with the correct notices served. It must have been in writing at the outset.
- All paperwork must be in order and available.
- Claims can be for possession and fixed costs only, NOT for rent arrears etc. (rent arrears and other costs can be sought in a separate claim, in the usual way). This is a major disadvantage of this procedure.

CHAPTER 16 - COURT ORDERS.

- This procedure can only be used against the original tenant. It may not matter if the tenancy has been renewed.
- A combined affidavit/application form must be completed and sworn by the landlord. This is in a prescribed form. The agreement and the relevant notices must be exhibited.
- The current Court fee is under £100, with "fixed" costs available if a Solicitor is employed by the landlord. The fixed Solicitor's costs are only a contribution towards the cost of the landlord's own Solicitor. Invariably the actual costs will be greater but these additional costs are not recoverable under this action.
- The Court will serve a copy of all documents on all defendants, which are treated as being served seven days after they are posted by the Court.
- The defendants must reply within 14 days from the date of service (effectively 21 days after the Court posted them).
- Where no reply is received from the defendants, within this 14 day period, the action will proceed as "un-contested". The plaintiff must file a written request for the possession order and the Court will put the papers before the Judge "without delay".
- Where a reply is received the Court Office will send a copy to the Plaintiff and refer the claim to the Judge.
- On receipt of the papers the Judge can either make an order for possession, or where he is not satisfied with the claim, will fix date for a Court Hearing.
- A notice of at least 14 days will be given to both parties of the date of the hearing.

RENT ARREARS

Claims for possession based on rent arrears must now be made to the Court using a prescribed form.

This applies whether or not possession is sought for some other reason as well.

CHAPTER 17 - INSTALLING THE TENANTS.

HOLDING DEPOSIT

Where a group of tenants has been chosen and the contract clauses agreed, the next step is to take from the tenants a holding deposit in order that the property is secured for them. This holding deposit should be in cleared funds in order that any cheques cannot be cancelled (see section on methods of payment).

The amount of the holding deposit should be an amount agreed by both parties to be the amount of loss likely to be incurred (by the landlord) should the tenant withdraw from signing contracts.

SERVICE AUTHORITIES

The services for the property should always be connected in the names of the person who is responsible for paying the bill. Where, for example, the tenant is responsible for paying the bill, the service should *always* be connected in the tenant's name. Any landlord who lets the supply remain in his own name will run the risk of having to pay any amount outstanding, should the tenant disappear. The service authority will chase the person who registered for the supply. Where the supply is in the tenant's name and they disappear without paying, the service authority may require a large deposit from the next person who registers, in order to prevent this happening again.

The prudent landlord should always secure from the tenants a deposit as security against damage to the property. The amount should be agreed by both parties, but would usually be in the region of one month's rent.

This deposit should be held by the landlord (or a third party) in trust for the tenants, pending the landlord's agreement that the property is in the same condition as it was when the tenants took possession (see section on inventory). Some landlords will pay interest on this deposit amount.

The condition of the property will be subject to normal wear and tear.

It should be made clear to the tenants at the commencement of the contract that this deposit is not to be used as the final month's rent for the property.

INFORMATION

The tenant should be provided with the full details of the landlord in order that he can communicate with him at any time. This is a legal requirement and the tenant can insist on this. He can write to the landlord's agent or the rent collector and ask for written details of the landlord or in the case of a company, details of the Director and secretary.

It is a criminal offence under the Landlord and Tenant Act 1985 not to comply with this request.

In the majority of circumstances the landlord will wish to know of any problems with the property at the earliest possible time, this way he can deal with these problems on a "stitch in time saves nine" basis. Indeed - how can a landlord repair anything unless he knows that it is broken.

COUNCIL TAX

The Council Tax is the current way in which the Local Authority charges for the local services, Police, Fire Brigade etc.

CHAPTER 17 - INSTALLING THE TENANTS.

It is a tax which is assessed on the individual property and is based on the market value of the property at a base date of April 1991. This given value falls into one of seven price bands and the tax is applied to each of these bands.

Those responsible for paying the Council Tax on a property, can be found from the following list. Reading from 1 to 6, "stop" as soon as you reach the description which fits the property. It is this person who is liable to pay the Council Tax, subject to what is explained below.

1. A resident freeholder.
2. A resident leaseholder (This includes assured Tenants under the Housing Act 1988)
3. A resident statutory or secure tenant.
4. A resident licensee.
5. A resident.
6. The owner (this applies where the property has no residents)

A resident is a person of 18 years or over who occupies the dwelling as their only or main residence.

Where either the property is let in parts (e.g. on separate tenancies of individual rooms) or under the circumstances where the property has been adapted or constructed for "multiple occupation" it is the owner/landlord who is liable to pay the Council Tax and the table set out above does not apply.

METHODS OF PAYMENT

There are many methods by which payments can be made. We will review some of them !

Cash - self explanatory, beware of forgeries and of receiving large amounts, especially where you are not near a bank to deposit it. !!

Personal cheques - These are a common form of money transfer as the majority of people have a bank account. Cheques can take up to five working days to "clear" through the banking system. It means that the transfer from one account to another is not completed for up to five days and can be refused or cancelled at any time within this period. The money will appear on your account in an "un-cleared" form but at this stage the amount can (and will) be removed if the cheque "bounces". Once the cheque has been cleared the money cannot be taken out of your account. Personal cheques can also be raised on certain types of Building Society account.
Where required the person who receives the cheque can ask the bank for "special clearance". There is a small charge for this service, but it will still take some 2/3 days for the cheque to "clear".

Banker's draft - These are available to any person with a bank account. They can be arranged at you own branch or through another branch of the same bank. The basis is that the bank will take the money out of your account when they issue the banker's draft - this guarantees that they will get their money. The banker's draft can be made out in the name of any person or company.
This banker's draft will take the same time to clear as a normal cheque, but the advantage is that it cannot be cancelled unless lost or stolen. Beware of forgeries and stolen banker's drafts - but these tend to be used by untraceable people purchasing an item from you (cars, boats etc.), not by tenants. There is also a small charge for this service.

Building Society Cheques - These are similar to banker's drafts in that the cheque is made out to a third party by the building society itself and it takes the money out of the person's account. Building society cheques take up to five days to become cleared funds. There is usually no charge for this.

Direct debit - a direct debit is an authority set up by the beneficiary on a personal account, whereby the account holder agrees to let the authorised person take money out of his account. This amount can be varied by the authorised person as and when necessary.

Standing order - A standing order is an instruction by the account holder to their banker to pay a certain amount of money into a specified account on a specific date, on a regular basis. This amount and instruction can only be altered by the account holder.

CHAPTER 17 - INSTALLING THE TENANTS.

CHAPTER 18 - MANAGING THE PROPERTY.

LANDLORD'S OBLIGATIONS

Under the 1985 Landlord and Tenant Act the landlord has certain obligations which he agrees to when he signs the agreement.

These obligations can be summed up as follows:-

- To keep in repair the structure and exterior of the property, this is to include all drains, gutters and external pipes.
- To keep in repair and proper working order the installations in the property for the supply of gas, water, electricity and sanitation, this is to include sinks, basins, baths and sanitary equipment, but not the fixtures, fittings or appliances for making use of the supplies.
- To keep in repair and proper working order the installations in the dwelling-house for space heating and heating water.

The landlord's obligations do not extend to works or repairs for which the tenant is liable by reason of his own duty to use the premises in a tenant-like manner.

The landlord's obligations have been extended significantly in respect of leases granted after 15th January 1989, under the 1988 Housing Act.

Where previously the landlord had an obligation to keep the structure and exterior of the premises in repair, this has been extended to "any part of the building in which the lessor (landlord) has an estate or interest" i.e. where the building is divided into different units the landlord has an obligation to keep the common parts in repair.

Where previously the landlord had an obligation to keep the installations for gas, electric and sanitation etc. in repair, this has been extended to "any installation which serves the property as long as the installation either forms part of any building which is under the landlord's control".

The landlord can only be made to carry out these extended repairs where it is affecting the tenant's enjoyment of the premises or common parts.

The landlord cannot be made to carry out these extended repairs where he requires access to areas of the building where he does not enjoy a right of access, so long as he has made all reasonable endeavours to do so.

Most disputes between landlord and tenant arise due to the general repair and maintenance of items in the property that are not specifically covered on the contract. Where, for example, a standard form of contract is used, responsibility is not always clear and where there are "grey areas" there are potential problems. It is therefore advisable for the agreement to be as specific as possible so that the "grey areas" are minimised.

Generally, where the tenants rents a property with certain items included (i.e. washing machine etc.) and there is no specific provision within the agreement covering maintenance of such appliances, the property can be considered as let as a "total package" complete with all the items included. The tenant takes on this "package" and the rent would have been set at a level to include the whole "package". The tenant could therefore argue that he has the right to expect that the items included in the "package" should be maintained in good order for the duration of the tenancy.

Therefore, the best advice is to use agreements where the responsibilities are clearly stated, so that there are no complications once the contract is in force.

CHAPTER 18 - MANAGING THE PROPERTY.

PROTECTION FROM EVICTION ACT 1977

It is an offence to take a person's home away from him unlawfully.

Under the 1977 Protection from Eviction Act it is an offence for a landlord to perform an act which is likely to interfere with the peace or comfort of a tenant, or any one living with him. This is extended to an act of withholding or withdrawing services to which the tenant is entitled.

The offence is to perform any of the above acts with the knowledge, intention, or having reasonable cause to believe, that this would make the tenant vacate, or stop using part of his home.

Anyone convicted under the 1977 Protection from Eviction Act will be fined or, in extreme cases, sent to prison.

The precise offences are set out in the Act which, have been made stronger by the Housing Act 1988.

TYPICAL HARASSMENT

Withdrawal of services - A landlord may be guilty of an offence if he persistently withdraws or withholds services which are necessary for the tenant to be able to live in his home.

Anti-social behaviour by the landlord or his agent - The Local Authority has power to prevent excessive noise under section 58 of the Control of Pollution Act 1974.

Failure to carry out repairs - The landlord has neglected the property so badly, he wants to drive the tenants out. Where the tenant has made reasonable approaches to the landlord and the landlord has failed to carry out the repairs the tenant may wish to take matters further. Local Authorities have powers to oblige a landlord to carry out repairs.

These powers apply to:-

- Major repairs.
- Minor but significant repairs.

A Local Authority may serve notice on a landlord requiring him to carry out repairs. If he fails to do so, the Local Authority may carry out the work itself.

Under the 1988 Housing Act, where a landlord is taken to Court for refusing to comply with the Local Authority repair notice, it will no longer be necessary to name the person who originally complained.

The Local Authority can now stipulate a start date and a completion date for the works so that the landlord does not delay, in the hope of driving the tenant out.

Threats and physical harassment - If a landlord uses threatening or violent language or physical behaviour against his tenant then an offence may have been committed. A tenant has obvious recourse to the police where there is actual physical assault. Where the harassment is so severe that it causes the tenant to leave the home, an offence will have been committed under the Protection of Eviction Act 1977.

CHAPTER 19 - PROBLEMS AND MAINTENANCE

GENERAL PROBLEMS

A good landlord must minimise the problems that may arise when letting a property and when they do arise he must act quickly to stop the cause and prevent the problem from happening again.

Most problems can be solved with a little thought and attention, for example:- Excess heat loss, frozen pipes, fire due to electrical wiring etc.

There are some problems which cannot be prevented but by acting quickly it is possible for the damage to be minimised, for example:- damp, rot etc.

It is important the landlord knows where to locate the following, and that the tenants are made fully aware of these locations, in case of emergencies:

- Water mains stop cock.
- Gas main stop cock.
- Electricity main switch.

Have a list of emergency phone numbers to hand. These should include some (if not all) of the following:

- The water board's emergency number.
- The gas board's emergency number.
- The electricity board's emergency number.
- A reliable electrician.
- A reliable plumber.
- A reliable general builder/odd job man.

A landlord should not tackle any job himself, unless he knows what he is doing. It is important that he uses qualified tradesmen. He should try to use someone who has done satisfactory work on a previous occasion for him or a friend and is a member of the appropriate professional body.

CHAPTER 19 - PROBLEMS AND MAINTENANCE

It is important to have a "house saving kit" at the tenants disposal, this should include the following:

- First aid box.
- Fire blankets.
- Fire extinguishers.
- Selection of fuses.
- Torch/candles.
- Basic tools i.e. screwdriver etc.

ELECTRICITY

Electricity meters come in two basic forms

- Pre-payment "key" meter.
- Quarterly meter.

Key meters are usually installed free and should have the added advantage that no deposit will be required by the Electricity Company. The customer will be provided with an electronic "key" which they take to a "charging station" to be credited with an amount of electricity. The customer decides how much they want to charge the key with (£5, £20, £50 etc.). The key is then placed in the meter and the meter is then credited with this amount, which can be used as required. The process is then repeated. This system has the advantage to the customer that the electricity is paid for before it is used and therefore no bill ever arrives. The electricity used is slightly more expensive than that of a quarterly bill, as there is no standing charge. The Electricity Company usually prefers this method as customers cannot leave the premises with large unpaid bills.

Quarterly bills are generated from standard meters which are easy to read and reading them enables the bill to be checked at regular intervals. The new style meters consist of a series of figures which corresponds to the amount of electric "units" used since the meter was installed. The old style of meter is a series of dials which have to be read in the right order to obtain the correct reading.

It is very important to have the house wiring circuit tested every five years. If the wiring is more than 25 years old, or if the socket outlets are of the round pin type, it almost certainly needs to be renewed.

A landlord should always call in expert help for electrical repairs and wiring (see section on electrical equipment safety regulations).

GAS

Where there is a smell of gas - act immediately, do not wait for others to act or ignore it hoping it will go away:-

- Extinguish all naked flames.
- Do not smoke.
- Opens doors and windows to enable the gas to escape. Leave them open until the problem has been solved.
- Where the cause cannot be located, or where the cause can be located but not easily dealt with, turn the gas off at the main gas tap. This is usually located outside the premises in a plastic box.
- Call the British Gas emergency number - under "GAS" in the telephone book.
- A qualified gas fitter will call around to deal with the problem. The check, the first thirty minutes of their time and any small parts will be provided free of charge. If the fault is on the road side of the installation, the whole of the works will be free. If in doubt ask the fitter what the likely costs will be.

All appliances which burn fossil fuel (i.e. gas, coal or oil) can produce carbon monoxide, if they have been fitted incorrectly or have not been serviced regularly (see section on gas safety regulations).

CHAPTER 19 - PROBLEMS AND MAINTENANCE

Carbon monoxide is a highly poisonous gas, and about 40 people die from it each year, most of these through faulty gas appliances.

It is a very difficult to detect as it has no colour, no taste and no smell.

It is therefore vital that all appliances are correctly installed and serviced by qualified personnel in accordance with the Gas Safety Regulations.

Carbon monoxide detectors are widely available and come in two types; "alarm" types retail at about £40-£50 and the coloured "patch" types are under £10. Consult your local hardware store for further details.

Only British Gas or a CORGI registered contractor may carry out work on a gas installation.

For further information contact British Gas (number in your local phone directory) or freephone 0800 181565 or CORGI on 01256 708133.

CHAPTER 20 - VACATING THE PROPERTY.

The landlord should not allow the deposit to be used up as the last month's rent. Where possible this should be included as a clause in the contract.

The property should be in the same condition at the end of the tenancy as it was at the commencement, less accepted wear and tear.

The landlord should make an appointment with the tenants to check the signed inventory. This will avoid any unnecessary disagreements. It is advisable that the deposit is returned to the tenants once the property has been vacated and the keys etc. returned.

The distinction between damage and wear and tear is something which is not easily quantifiable and both the landlord and the tenant should be prepared to discuss and negotiate this. It should be linked to the period of time that the tenants were in occupation at the premises along with the age of the furnishings.

When the tenants are vacating the premises they will usually request that the supplies are taken from their names as they will no longer want to be responsible for the bills.

The landlord should try to ensure that these are connected into his name in order to avoid having to pay any reconnection charges.

Where there are tenants who are moving in straight away, the supplies should obviously be connected into their names.

Each time a property is vacated the landlord should think about replacing the locks in order that the security of the premises is not compromised.

The landlord should make sure that the property is secure once the tenants have vacated.

CHAPTER 20 - VACATING THE PROPERTY.

Doors, windows etc. Should all be firmly closed to avoid access by potential “squatters”. The cost of removing such squatters through the Courts is high, when this is coupled with the loss of rental income for the period that they are in occupation, the final cost can be astronomical !!.

The whole letting process can be repeated for new tenants.

CHAPTER 21 - FURTHER INFORMATION.

SMALL LANDLORD'S ASSOCIATION

The Small Landlord's Association is the national organisation for landlords' of residential property.

The SLA was founded in 1973 by Mrs Lilian Cline. It is a non-profit making organisation run on a largely voluntary basis by a committee of landlords, whose concern for their members stems from their own experience. It is affiliated to the British Property Federation, which is the national organisation concerned with the whole spectrum of property issues.

The Associations aims are:-

- to safeguard and promote the private sector's role in housing the nation.
- To represent to the government the views of the private landlord on current and future legislation.
- To ensure that landlords are aware of their statutory rights under current legislation.
- To represent the views of landlords to Local Authorities, and to monitor the performance of Local Authorities in carrying out their statutory obligations to landlords and tenants.
- To promote the good name of the private rented sector through the media, and to counter misrepresentation.
- To foster a fair and friendly relationship between landlord and tenant.

The SLA provides membership benefits in the following ways:-

- A regular newsletter which is available nationally, whose contents are solely directed at the private residential landlord.
- Advice on the complex legislation surrounding all aspects of housing, and a resource of case studies in areas of law that are poorly defined.

CHAPTER 21 - FURTHER INFORMATION.

- Advice on matters relating to environmental health regulations, and on housing benefit.
- Advice on the implementation of all relevant regulations, including gas safety, fire and furnishing regulations.
- Advice on insurance and taxation.
- Regular meetings addressed by leading figures from organisations concerned with residential property.
- The distribution to members of all official information leaflets and booklets, and advice on their interpretation.

Membership applications are welcomed from all private landlords: from those who just let one room in their house, and from those who have a street of houses. The membership subscription is kept extremely low, and further details may be obtained from:-

The Membership Secretary,
Small Landlord's Association,
53 Werter Road
London SW15 2LL.

Tel: 0181 780 9954.

CHAPTER 22 - RECOMMENDED HELP.

For further information and/or advice try contacting the following, who have helped in the preparation of this guide:

ACCOUNTANT
G Christodoulou
Gilchrists
Certified Accountants/Registered Auditors
West Hill House
6 Swains Lane
Highgate
London N6 6QU
Tel: 0171 482 4212
Fax: 0171 267 4382

INSURANCE
For up to date insurance information contact:
Alpha Lets (UK) Ltd
371 Green Lanes
London N4 1DY
Tel: 0181 800 4313
Fax: 0181 800 4887

SOLICITOR
R O Jones
Bury Walkers
4 Butts Court
Leeds LS1 5JS
Tel: 0113 244 4227
Fax: 0113 246 5965

ASSOCIATION OF RESIDENTIAL LETTING AGENTS
18/21 Jermyn Street
London SW1 6HP
Tel: 0171 734 0655

NATIONAL ASSOCIATION OF ESTATE AGENTS
Arbon House
21 Jury Street

Warwick CV34 4EH
Tel: 01926 496800
Fax: 01926 400953

SMALL LANDLORDS' ASSOCIATION
53 Werter Road
London SW15 2LL
Tel: 0181 780 9954
Fax: 0181 780 1302

STANDARD FORMS OF CONTRACT
Oyez Stationery Group
144/146 Fetter Lane
London EC4A 1BT
Tel: 0171 405 2847
Fax: 0171 242 9318

LETTING AGENTS & PROPERTY MANAGERS
Alpha-Lets (UK)Ltd
371 Green Lanes
London N4 1DY
Tel: 0181 809 6144
Fax: 0181 800 4887

ROYAL INSTITUTION OF CHARTERED SURVEYORS
12 Great George Street
London SW1P 3AD
Tel: 0171 222 7000
Fax: 0171 334 3722

MAIL-ORDER CONTRACTS
Alpha-Lets (UK) Ltd
371 Green Lanes
London N4 1DY
Tel: 0181 800 4313
Fax: 0181 800 4887

CHAPTER 23 - TYPICAL QUESTIONS

Here are some typical questions which are commonly asked, along with their appropriate answers.

- I have heard that you have to "serve" the notices on tenants, how exactly do you "serve" notices. Can they be posted ? If so, is ordinary post all right, or should it be Recorded Delivery ? If they are "served" by hand, does it need to be witnessed ?

  Unless there is some provision in the contract or one of the statutory rules apply you must show that the notice came into the tenant's hands or otherwise came to the tenant's attention by the requisite date. A well drawn tenancy agreement should make provision for how notices are served including those notices which have to be given under the Housing Act 1988. However, as it is not always easy to prove service in court, it is much better if the notice can be handed to the tenant with a witness present. If the agreement allows for service by post then the Recorded Delivery service should be used. The agreement may also allow for the notice to be left at the property, addressed to the tenant; if so this method can be used.

- I have a six month AST with my tenants which was signed last month, they now tell me they have to leave, can they do this ? Do they need to give any "notice" ? There is no mention of any of this in my agreement.

  There is nothing with the Housing Act 1988 which deals specifically with the tenants rights/obligations when giving notice. However, in the absence of a "break-clause" in the agreement which allows the tenant to give early notice, the tenant has a duty to pay rent for the duration of the fixed term.

- I have a six month AST with my tenants which was signed seven months ago and has now become a statutory periodic tenancy. The tenants had agreed to remain indefinitely, but they now tell me they have to leave tomorrow, can they do this ? Do they need to give any "notice" ?

  Yes - notice of the same length as a period of tenancy must be given, subject to a minimum of four weeks. This must run out on the rent day or the day before. For example, with a monthly statutory periodic tenancy at least one month's notice must be given, expiring in this way.

- I have a twelve month AST and I am not happy with my tenants, who moved in seven months ago, even though they have not specifically done anything wrong. Can I get possession of the property back ?. The "Section 20 Notice" seems to indicate that I can, in that it says:
  "Provided that you keep to the terms of the tenancy, you are entitled to remain at the dwelling for the <u>first six</u> months <u>of</u> the fixed period agreed at the start of the tenancy."

  No - you can only rely on Section 21 of the 1988 Housing Act to evict the tenant once the contractual term (in this case 12 months) has run out. At least two months notice is required.

- I have a 12 month AST with three joint tenants which has 4 months left to run, one wants to leave and he has found a suitable replacement. I don't want to draw up a new six month agreement. Can the tenant be replaced on the *original* agreement ?

Where all the parties to the original agreement (and the new tenant) approve, it is possible to make a change. A written agreement should be drawn up stating that all parties (including the landlord) agree to the change and that all parties understand that the original tenancy is to continue and that the new tenant will be taking over all the rights and obligations of the tenant being replaced. This agreement should be signed by all parties: i.e. the landlord, the original tenants (including the one leaving) and the new tenant.

- What rights does a person who is not on the contract (i.e. a boyfriend) have, if the original tenant remains at the property ?

  Where the original tenant remains at the property, a person who is not on the agreement has a licence from the tenant to be in the property, assuming that there is no clause in the tenancy agreement prohibiting such occupation. A clause prohibiting sub-letting does not suffice to prevent such occupations.

- What rights does a person who is not on the contract (i.e. a boyfriend) have, if the original tenant disappears ?

  Where the original tenant has disappeared from the property, a person who is not on the agreement has no rights over the property under the agreement, once the agreement comes to an end. However, should they refuse to leave, the landlord cannot remove them by force, but must get a Court Order to obtain vacant possession.

CHAPTER 23 - TYPICAL QUESTIONS

- My tenants have people "visiting" the property all the time, is this allowed ? If so, how often and for how long can they stay ?

  There is no prescribed time limit for visitors to a property. If you have objections it is better to limit such activities by including a clause within the letting agreement.

- I have a six month AST which was signed in March 1990, I didn't terminate the contract and it has lapsed into a "statutory periodic contract" how long will this continue without giving the tenants security of tenure.

  The agreement will continue indefinitely without the tenants having any long-term rights, but be careful to keep copies of the agreement in a safe place in case you need to prove that the original agreement was indeed an AST.

- I have heard that there is a price limit for an AST, my property in Kensington is valued at £3500 per month, can I use an AST for this property ?

  A tenancy with a rent of £25,000 or more per annum cannot be an Assured Tenancy (and therefore cannot be an Assured Shorthold Tenancy). The tenant's rights will depend upon the terms of the contract.

- I have tenants who want to stay in my property for eight years and I want to draw up an AST for this fixed eight year period. Can I do this, or is there a time limit for the fixed term ?

CHAPTER 23 - TYPICAL QUESTIONS

There is no time limit for the fixed term of an AST. However, it is inadvisable because if the tenant successfully applies to the Rent Assessment Committee for a determination that the rent is significantly in excess of the market rent, this will remain in effect for the full period of the fixed term i.e. up to eight years. !!

- A tenant of mine has informed me that he works from home. I have no objections to this but the AST says that he should not carry on a profession or trade from the premises. Am I exposing myself to any risk because I allow this to take place ?

  An AST cannot be granted on a business premises, however it would be dependant on what work is taking place at the premises. Where a tenant is (say) a writer and he works from what is his principal, primary residence, there should be no problem.
  Permission should not be granted where he has customers etc. visiting the premises.

- I have a furnished AST and the washing machine that I provided has broken down. It is only 18 months old and I am suspicious that the tenants have being misusing it. Am I responsible for repairing it ?

  Where there is no provision for its maintenance and repair within the agreement neither party will be responsible.
  The tenants may be able to argue, successfully, that there is an implied obligation on the landlord to repair the washing machine as the rent includes payment for the benefit of using it.

However, if the appliance has been damaged due to the negligence of the tenants it would be their responsibility to pay for the repairs.

- I have five tenants on a joint tenancy and one of them has "disappeared", leaving his room empty. The other four tenants are refusing to pay for the fifth person, saying that they only have to pay their own portion, is this so ?

The tenants are not correct if they are on a joint tenancy agreement as this makes them "jointly and severally liable" i.e. they are all responsible for the total amount of the rent between them. You can therefore, chase one or all of them for the full rent.

CHAPTER 24 - GLOSSARY OF TERMS

Certain terminology has been used within this guide. A brief explanation of some of this terminology is set out below:-

Act of Parliament - a law made by Parliament; a statute.

Action - where a person seeks to enforce his rights via the Courts.

Agent - a person who has been given authority to act on behalf of another.

Assignment - the transferring of the interests of one tenant under a lease, to another.

Calendar month - period of time from the same date in consecutive months (see later for full explanation)

Common law - the law of England and Wales, added to by Judges' decisions, as opposed to statute.

Contract - a legally binding agreement.

Covenants - promises between landlords and tenants to carry out certain duties, i.e. obligations under a lease. These can be expressed or implied by statute.

County Courts - the courts which deal with smaller civil cases.

Criminal Law - the Law which concerns the community as a whole.

Deposit (repairs) - a sum of money held by the landlord for the tenant pending any damages or expenses caused to the landlord by the tenant. This deposit should be fully refundable, less these agreed deductions.

CHAPTER 24 - GLOSSARY OF TERMS

Deposit (holding) - an amount of money held by the landlord from the tenant to secure the property on behalf of the tenant. This would usually be some sort of part payment and the tenant should confirm whether this sum is refundable, or not. In law part payments are usually fully refundable but there may compensation to pay to the landlord for the cancellation. To avoid problems it is prudent that both parties agree whether this holding deposit is refundable should either side not sign contracts.

Determination - the end of an interest in land.

Estate - an interest in land by a person.

Exclusive possession - the right to exclude all others from the premises. This includes the landlord.

Fee - a sum of money charged by the landlord which will usually be a premium or deposit. Accommodation agencies sometimes charge tenants a fee for finding accommodation which is taken up. It is, however, illegal for an accommodation agency to charge a fee for just providing tenants with a list of property details or for registering details of someone seeking a tenancy.

Granting - transferring or giving.

Joints tenants - two or more people who have the same rights to the same property.

Landlord - the owner of the property who grants the lease.

Lease - written contract for the letting of a property.

Licence - the right granted by a landlord to a tenant to use a property without the tenant obtaining a tenancy.

CHAPTER 24 - GLOSSARY OF TERMS

MIRAS - Mortgage Interest Relief At Source.

Possession action - attempting to recover the property from the tenant via the courts.

Premium - An amount of money charged to the tenant at the beginning of the contract. This will give the tenant the right to assign the tenancy, unless prohibited under the agreement.

Prescribed (form) - where the law requires that a particular wording is used in a form; otherwise the form will not be valid.

Re-entry - retaking possession of a property.

Residential occupier - the use of a property as a home.

Self-contained - a dwelling which has all its own facilities and has a means of being separated from other dwellings by a single door.

Service charge - Charge, usually levied in a block of flats, for works to communal areas.

Statute - an Act of Parliament.

Tenant - the person to whom the lease is granted.

CALCULATION OF RENTS ON A CALENDAR MONTH BASIS

Calendar month - a period of time from the same date in each month, for example from the 10th day of May to the 9th day of June. This period may thus vary in length from month to month. It is calculated by multiplying the weekly rent by 52 (weeks per year) and dividing by 12 (months per year) e.g. for a weekly rent of £120.00, the monthly rent is £520.00

£120.00 x 52/12 = £520.00

This period is not to be confused with a four weekly period which would make a payment of £480.00 every four weeks.

£120.00 x 4 = £480.00

However, the four weekly period would be paid thirteen times per year, whereas, the monthly payment is only paid twelve times per year.

Thus the payments over a year would be identical e.g.

12 x £520.00 = £ 6240.00

13 x £480.00 = £ 6240.00

This is usually done to help those who are on a monthly salary (12 x per year).

If a tenant receives a monthly salary and pays his rent "four weekly" (13 x per year) at some stage in the year two rent payments will fall within one salary payment.

A four week month is also called a lunar month.

INDEX

INDEX